The Library of Southern Civilization

Lewis P. Simpson, Editor

REMINISCENCES OF CONFEDERATE SERVICE

REMINISCENCES

OF

CONFEDERATE

SERVICE

1861-1865

FRANCIS W. DAWSON

EDITED BY BELL I. WILEY
WITH AN INTRODUCTION, AN APPENDIX,
AND NOTES

LOUISIANA STATE UNIVERSITY PRESS
BATON ROUGE AND LONDON

LIBRARY OF CONGRESS CATALOGING IN PUBLICATION DATA

Dawson, Francis W.
  Reminiscences of Confederate service, 1861–1865.

  (The Library of Southern civilization)
  Includes bibliographical references.
    1. Dawson, Francis W. 2. United States—History—Civil War, 1861–
  1865—Personal narratives—Confederate side. 3. Confederate States of
  America. Army. Department of Northern Virginia—Biography. 4. United
  States—History—Civil War, 1861–1865—Regimental histories—Department
  of Northern Virginia. I. Wiley, Bell Irvin, 1906–   II. Title.
  E605.D27   1980   973.7'82   79-26720
  ISBN 0-8071-0689-5 (cloth)
  ISBN 0-8071-1885-0 (paper)

Louisiana Paperback Edition, 1993

02 01 00 99 98 97 96 95 94 93   5 4 3 2 1

CONTENTS

INTRODUCTION

FRANCIS WARRINGTON DAWSON was an unusual person. Born in London, May 20, 1840, he was christened Austin John Reeks. His father, Joseph Austin Reeks, and his mother, Mary Perkins Reeks were reduced to near poverty by the father's financial speculations. Through the assistance of a widowed aunt, he received a good preparatory education, but he did not go to college. He toured the continent as a youth, and before he was twenty he showed considerable promise as a playwright. He was fair complexioned, curly haired, and handsome.

In the latter part of 1861, after deciding to emigrate to America to enter Confederate service, he changed his name to Francis Warrington Dawson. His choice of a name was influenced by his admiration of an uncle, William A. Dawson, an English army captain killed in India, whose widow had helped finance the youth's education.

With the assistance of A. Dudley Mann, Confederate agent in England, Dawson persuaded Captain Robert B. Pegram, commanding officer of the Confederate States steamer the *Nashville,* then at Southampton obtaining supplies for the South, to let him join the *Nashville*'s crew in the capacity of a common sailor. During the voyage from Southampton to Beaufort, North Carolina, in January–February, 1862, Dawson ingratiated himself with Pegram and other officers. Shortly after arriving in the South, Pegram had Dawson commissioned as a master's mate in the Confederate Navy. In the spring of 1862 Pegram was appointed to command the ironclad *Louisiana,* then nearing completion at New Orleans. He and Dawson in April started to New Orleans; but just before they reached their destination they learned of the fall of New Orleans and the destruction of the *Louisiana*.

Dawson was convinced that shortage of war vessels and surplus of personnel would make it difficult for him to see active service as a naval officer. On his return to Richmond he attached himself as a volunteer to Purcell's battery of field artillery commanded by Captain Willie B. Pegram, nephew of Robert B. Pegram. In the battle of Mechanicsville, June 26, 1862, while bravely serving as a member of the gun crew, he was wounded in the leg. Reports of his gallantry came to the attention of Mrs. G. W. Randolph, wife of the Confederate secretary of war and a cousin of Robert B. Pegram. Through the good offices of Robert Pegram and Mrs. Randolph and on the recommendation of Captain Willie Pegram, Dawson was commissioned first lieutenant of artillery. He was assigned to duty as an assistant ordnance officer on the staff of General James Longstreet. Just before the battle of Antietam he was captured and sent to Fort Delaware. After three weeks he was released on parole. He visited friends in the Petersburg area until he was exchanged late in November, 1862. He rejoined Longstreet's staff on December 6, 1862, at Fredericksburg. Dawson's comments on the engagement are brief, but he described in some detail snowball fights, poker games, and other diversions of the several weeks in winter quarters that followed the battle.

Early in 1863 Longstreet was placed in command of the Department of Virginia and North Carolina, with headquarters at Petersburg. In the subsequent attempt to capture Suffolk, Longstreet was unsuccessful. He rejoined Lee after Chancellorsville and in June moved with the Army of Northern Virginia to Pennsylvania.

Dawson's account of Gettysburg is brief but interesting. In September he went with Longstreet's corps to north

Georgia, but did not reach his destination in time to participate in the battle of Chickamauga. Bragg unwisely
sent Longstreet to Knoxville early in November to try
to drive the Federals out of that city. Thus Bragg was
deprived of Longstreet's assistance in the disastrous battles at Chattanooga, November 23–25. On November 29
Longstreet made an unsuccessful attack on Burnside's
forces at Knoxville. He then marched eastward to Russellville, Tennessee, where the army went into winter quarters. Dawson gives some details of the hardships endured by
the Confederates during this period. "The men suffered
frightfully," he wrote. "It is no exaggeration to say that
on such marches as they were obliged to make in that bitter weather they left the bloody tracks of their feet on
the sharp stones of the roads."

After Christmas, Dawson went to Richmond for several
weeks of leave. Shortly after his return to duty he was examined for promotion; he passed the examination and
received his captain's commission on April 2, 1864.

Later in April, Longstreet was ordered to rejoin Lee's
army at Gordonsville. Dawson gives a vivid account of
the Wilderness fighting on May 6, and of the serious
wounding of Longstreet on that day. The young Britisher
became a good friend of Longstreet's temporary successor,
General R. H. Anderson, but, with the exception of Colonel P. T. Manning, chief of ordnance, he found little
congeniality with members of the I Corps staff. "The staff
had 'no use' for me," he wrote, "which was perhaps not
surprising as I was a stranger and a foreigner." In November, 1864, he was happy to accept appointment as ordnance officer on the staff of General Fitzhugh Lee, who,
in January, 1865, succeeded Wade Hampton as commander of the cavalry corps of the Army of Northern Virginia.

Of Longstreet, Dawson wrote perceptively: "The reputation that Longstreet had as a fighting man was unquestionably deserved, and when in action, there was no lack of energy or of quickness of perception, but he was somewhat sluggish by nature, and I saw nothing in him to make me believe that his capacity went beyond the power to conduct a square hard fight. The power of combination he did not possess, and whenever he had an independent command, he was unsuccessful. . . . It should be said of Longstreet, especially in view of his political course since the war, that he never faltered or hesitated in his devotion to the Confederate cause."

Dawson found service with Fitzhugh Lee's cavalry hard but interesting. He was especially appreciative of the kindness shown by Lee to his staff: "We were always treated as if we were his kinsmen."

After the surrender of R. E. Lee, Dawson decided to remain in the South. As a paroled Confederate he could not leave the country. But, as he wrote his mother, he wanted to stay in America, anyhow, because he thought opportunities for getting ahead were good. He obtained employment with the Richmond *Examiner* for a while and then with the *Dispatch*. In November, 1866, he went to Charleston, South Carolina, where he worked first with the *Mercury* and then with the *News,* the latter a paper in which he and his friend B. R. Riordan bought a major interest in 1868. In 1873 Dawson and Riordan also acquired the *Courier* and merged their two papers into the *News and Courier.*

In the meantime Dawson took out naturalization papers; on April 1, 1868, he became a citizen of the United States. In 1867 he married Virginia Fourgeaud, of Charleston; she died in 1873 of tuberculosis. In 1874 he married Sarah Morgan, sister of his long-time friend, James Morris Morgan. Sarah Dawson was a talented woman from Louisiana, who in 1913 was to become the author of *A*

Confederate Girl's Diary. She was thirty-one when she married Dawson and a semiinvalid from a spinal injury received when she fell from a carriage during the Civil War. Dawson treated his wife with great tenderness, and their marriage apparently was a happy one. They had three children, the youngest of whom died in infancy. The middle child, Frank Warrington Dawson II, born September 27, 1878, was for many years an attaché at the American Embassy in Paris.

Francis Warrington Dawson in the 1870s and 1880s made the Charleston *News and Courier* one of the leading newspapers of the South. His most important work was his crusade for the industrialization of his adopted region. Pushing the slogan Bring the Cotton Mills to the Cotton, he did much to expand the textile business in South Carolina. He advocated diversification, scientific farming, and other progressive practices to improve the lot of the rural classes. He was a principal spokesman for the aristocratic Bourbon group, but he was more liberal than many of his associates, and he never was blinded to the interests and welfare of the masses. In 1880 he launched a vigorous and a successful campaign against dueling in South Carolina, and this subjected him to charges of cowardice. But he was a man of great courage, a fact that he repeatedly demonstrated during the war and afterward. He exposed and condemned the waste and corruption of the Radical Republicans in South Carolina. Much to the disgust of fellow Democrats, he supported Republican governor Daniel H. Chamberlain for a time in 1876 because of his belief that Chamberlain was trying to clean up the Republican party in South Carolina. But Dawson quickly shifted to Wade Hampton when the latter was nominated by the Democrats, and his strong editorial support was a factor in Hampton's election.

After the overthrow of the Radicals in 1877 Dawson played a prominent role in Democratic activities both on the local and national level. He wrote platforms and campaign literature for the state Democratic organization, and in 1880, 1884, and 1888 he served as a delegate to the National Democratic Convention. His support of Cleveland in 1884 led to the appointment of his brother-in-law, James Morgan, as consul-general to Australia.

Dawson's brilliant career came to a premature and tragic end on March 12, 1889. On that day he went to the office of a neighbor, Dr. T. B. McDow, to protest what he regarded as the doctor's improper advances to Dawson's Swiss maid, Marie Burdayron. During the brief altercation that ensued Dawson was fatally shot. His death brought a flood of tributes from throughout the country. Samuel Bowles, editor of the Springfield *Republican,* wrote on March 13: "As a journalist Captain Dawson had no superior in the South. His instincts were noble and he had that high devotion to his profession which made a well-balanced paper fill the full measure of his ambition."

On the same day Henry W. Grady of the Atlanta *Constitution* wrote: "Capt. Dawson was a masterful man. . . . South Carolina is a better and a more prosperous state because he lived in it and gave his life freely and daily to her service."

In 1882, seven years before his death, Dawson published *Reminiscences of Confederate Service, 1861–1865* in an edition of one hundred copies for private circulation. Copies of this book are very scarce. The one reproduced here is from the Library of the University of South Carolina.

The book is important not only because it is the record of an unusually observant and articulate man, but also because it is the only book-length memoir of an English officer in Confederate service.

The eighteen wartime letters, generously made available by the Duke University Library, are included as an appendix because of the additional detail that they contain, and because they have a spontaneity and exuberance not found in the reminiscences. I have made only minor changes in spelling, capitalization, and punctuation in these letters.

In preparing the new edition I had the help of Miss Mattie Russell of the Duke University Library, who provided Xerox copies of the Dawson letters, and of Dean S. Frank Logan, Wofford College, who generously loaned me a copy of his M.A. thesis "Francis W. Dawson, 1840–1889: South Carolina Editor" (Duke University, 1947). I also benefited from reading the sketch of Dawson in Jonathan Daniels, *They Will Be Heard: America's Crusading Newspaper Editors* (New York: McGraw-Hill Book Company, 1965).

REMINISCENCES

OF

CONFEDERATE SERVICE,

1861–1865.

BY

CAPT. FRANCIS W. DAWSON, C. S. A.

[100 COPIES.]

CHARLESTON, S. C.
THE NEWS AND COURIER BOOK PRESSES.
1882.

I.

It was in the autumn of 1861 that I made up my mind to go to the Southern States of America, and enter the Confederate Army. Looking back more than twenty years, I find it difficult, as the man of forty-two, to recall the exact feelings of the boy of twenty. I can say, however, that I had no expectation whatever of any gain, or advantage to myself. I had a sincere sympathy with the Southern people in their struggle for independence, and felt that it would be a pleasant thing to help them to secure their freedom. It was not expected, at that time, that the war would last many months, and my idea simply was to go to the South, do my duty there as well as I might, and return home to England. I expected no reward and wanted none, and had no intention whatever of remaining permanently in the Southern States.

There was much difficulty, of course, in obtaining accurate information as to the best way of reaching the seat of war in the South. I found that I could probably go by way of Nassau, N. P., but the expense would have been greater than I cared to incur, and the other mode of entering the Confederacy—by going to a Northern port and slipping through the lines—was exceedingly troublesome, and was, besides, uncertain in its result. However, I determined to go in some fashion, and just about this time the Confederate States steamer *Nashville* arrived at Southampton. This vessel had been one of the regular steamers on the line between Charleston and New York, and was seized, I believe, by the Confederate authorities after hostilities began. It had been determined to send the Hon. James M. Mason and the Hon. John Slidell to represent the Confederate

States in England and France respectively, and the *Nashville* was fitted out for the purpose of taking them to England. They changed their plan, unfortunately for them, and went in a small vessel to Havana, where they took the mail steamer *Trent* for St. Thomas. The trip of the *Nashville* was not, however, abandoned, and, under command of Captain Robert B. Pegram, she ran the blockade at Charleston and reached Southampton in safety, capturing and destroying during the voyage a fine American ship named the *Harvey Birch*.

The arrival of the *Nashville* at Southampton caused considerable stir. By those who were friendly to the North she was spoken of as a pirate, and her officers and crew were dubbed buccaneers. While some of the newspapers were disposed to order out Captain Pegram and his crew for instant execution, there were others which were quite friendly in tone. I remember that it became necessary for Captain Pegram to write a letter to " *The Times*," in which he explained that, far from being "a pirate," he was a regularly commissioned officer of the Confederate States Navy, and that the *Nashville* was a vessel of war of the Confederate States, entitled to the consideration that would be shewn to the war vessel of any other Government. This view was taken by the English authorities, although, under the proclamation of neutrality which the Queen had issued, the *Nashville* was not allowed to obtain any sort of equipment which could, by any stretch of the imagination, be conceived to be capable of use in war. The authorities at Southampton were so strict in their construction of the neutrality proclamation that they objected to our strengthening the forward deck, lest it might increase the efficiency of the vessel for fighting purposes. No repairs were allowed to be made except such as would place the *Nashville* in the precise condition in which she was when she left Charleston. The passage had been rough, or no repairs of the kind allowed would have been necessary. *Punch*, of course, made fun of the whole business, and had some rhyming verses on the subject, in which the name of Captain Pegram, the commander of the *Nashville*, was made to rhyme with "megrim."

It occurred to me that if I could in any way secure a passage to the South on the *Nashville*, it would be much better than trying to get there by way of Nassau or the Potomac. A man named Smith, to whom I was introduced in London by a friend, and who told me that a near kinsman of his was at that time, or had been, Governor of Arkansas, gave me a letter of introduction to Mr. North, who was one of the Confederate agents in London. I saw Mr. North and told him what I wanted, but I do not think that I made a very favorable impression. It seemed to him so extravagant a project that he evidently doubted my sincerity and honesty of purpose. The most that I could accomplish was to obtain from him a note introducing me to Captain Pegram. This was something gained, and a few days afterwards I went to Southampton.

As I neared my destination, I was surprised to find how large a share of public attention was given to the Confederate vessel. The appearance of the *Nashville*, her size, her speed, and the probable plans of her commander were diligently canvassed by those traveling with me, and I was gratified to find that every one had a good opinion of the conduct and character of the officers and crew of the vessel. Upon my arrival I went at once to the docks, and far in the distance saw a flag which was entirely new and strange. As

I drew nearer I found that it was flying from the peak of a large paddle-wheel steamer, painted black, and with more upper-works than I had been accustomed to see on sea-going vessels. The flag that I had seen was the Stars and Bars of the Confederacy, and the vessel was the *Nashville*. I went aboard and to my great annoyance was told that Captain Pegram was in London. The officer on duty was very courteous and disposed to be communicative, and I had a long talk with him. This officer was Lieutenant John J. Ingraham, of Charleston, S. C. I learned that he was a graduate of the Naval Academy at Annapolis, and it rather daunted me to be told that one could not expect to attain the rank of officer in the Navy unless one had had the thorough training of a naval school, or practical education at sea.

Some days later I went down to Southampton again, and this time saw Captain Pegram. The sweetness and dignity of his manner impressed me at once, and I unbosomed myself to him without reserve. I may mention here that he had been twenty-five or thirty years in the Navy when Virginia seceded from the Union, and instantly resigned his commission to share the fortunes of his native State. In his profession he had already gained distinction, and I have seen the sword of honor presented to him by the State of Virginia in recognition of his gallantry in an engagement with pirates in the Chinese Seas. On the golden scabbard of this sword his name and rank are engraved, with this simple but eloquent inscription:

" *The State of Virginia to a devoted son.*"

It need not be said that Captain Pegram was exceedingly kind and patient, but he told me frankly that it was impossible for him to do what I wished. He said: " I have no office which I can give you, and this being a Government vessel, I cannot take you as a passenger." Afterwards, I learned that some of the officers suggested that I might be a " Yankee spy " endeavoring to get into a position where I should be able to report the movements of the *Nashville* to her anxious friends on the other side. Amongst other things, Captain Pegram told me that there would be plenty of opportunities of reaching the South, as the United States would certainly refuse to surrender Messrs. Mason and Slidell [who had been taken from the English mail steamer *Trent* by Captain Wilkes of the *San Jacinto*, on November 8th, 1861], and that England's first act after declaring war would be to raise the blockade of the Southern ports. In spite of Captain Pegram's refusal, I persisted in urging him to take me, and at last he said: " There is only one thing that can be done; if you like to go as a sailor before the mast I will take you, but of course you will not dream of doing that." My answer was " I will do it ; and I hope that you will let me know when you are about to sail, in order that I may be here in time." Captain Pegram told me that he would do this, but either forgot it or supposed that my intentions must have changed when I realized what I had undertaken. But I did not realize it, and I did not change my mind. I ought to say here that, although I was twenty-one years old at this time, I did not look more than seventeen or eighteen, which will account for the habit that Captain Pegram has had of saying that I was a mere boy at the time that he made my acquaintance.

I returned to London, and began at once to make arrangements for my departure. My friend from Arkansas told me that the one indispensable thing was a bowie-knife, and he

explained the divers uses to which this weapon could be
put, assuring me that I would have no difficulty in seizing
the gun of a Yankee soldier by the muzzle and, with one dex-
terous blow, severing the barrel in twain. Another way of
using it was to attach a cord to the handle of this bowie-
knife and, with a skillful throw, to drive the blade into the
heart of the advancing foeman, and, when he should have
fallen, to haul it back by the string, and repeat the operation
on another of the enemy. I had not much faith in my
ability to use the bowie-knife in this fashion, but I ordered
one to be made by a surgical instrument maker, according to
a pattern given me by my Arkansas friend. A sanguinary
looking weapon it was. The blade was fifteen inches long and
about three inches wide, at the broadest part, and a third of
an inch thick at the back. I provided myself with a sea-chest,
which, according to Marryatt's novels, was indispensable to
a sea-faring man, caused my name to be painted on it in big
white letters, and held myself in readiness to start. But no
summons came. The papers would occasionally say that the
Nashville was to sail in a day or two, and I had many a false
alarm. Tired of waiting, I bade good-bye to my people at
home, and went down to Southampton, determined to
remain there until the time for going aboard should come.

At Southampton I purchased a sailor's outfit, and, when
I had rigged myself out in what I considered the proper
style, I went down to the vessel. I wore a blue woolen
shirt open at the neck ; a black silk handkerchief, with ample
flowing ends, tied loosely around the neck ; blue trousers,
made very tight at the knee and twenty-two inches in cir-
cumference at the bottom, and on my head a flat cloth cap
ornamented with long black ribbons. I had besides, in the
famous sea-chest, a pea jacket, sea boots, and the necessary

underclothing. As a reminder of my former estate, I retained a suit of dress clothes, and a black Inverness cape which I had been in the habit of wearing.

2

II.

As well as I can remember, it was on New Year's Day, 1862, that I went aboard the *Nashville*.

I reported to the officer of the deck, and told him that I had been ordered by Captain Pegram to come aboard for duty. I was turned over to the boatswain, who told me to go down into the "foksle." Up to this time I was supposed to be, what I appeared to be, a sailor. As a matter of fact my experience in nautical affairs had been confined to sailing miniature yachts on the Serpentine in Hyde Park, but I thought I had considerable theoretical knowledge obtained from the romances of Marryatt and Chamier, and Dana's excellent book: "*Two Years Before the Mast.*"

Following my conductor, Mr. Sawyer, I tumbled down the "companion," and found myself in as pleasant a place for being uncomfortable, as any one could desire.

The foksle, or forecastle, was about ten feet long, about five feet six inches high, and about ten feet broad aft, and six feet forward. The lack of height was an advantage to me, as when the vessel rolled I could hold on with my head and have my hands at liberty. On each side of the forecastle were the bunks or "rabbit hutches" for the crew. In the centre was a small table supported against the windlass bitt, a heavy piece of timber which passed through the forecastle. Around the bitt were hung a number of one-pronged forks, notched knives, and battered spoons, matching each other in only one thing—dirt. Twelve o'clock or "eight bells" rang, and the crew came down to dinner. There were but eight seamen on the *Nashville*, and they represented almost as many different nations. There was an Irishman, and a

Belgian, a North Carolinian and a Swede, a fat Cockney Englishman and a Frenchman, a Scotchman and a Spaniard. I found them to be mean, treacherous and obscene, and I shall say no more about them than is absolutely necessary. The dinner on the first day will serve as a sample of our usual diet, and of the crew's habitual behavior. First, there was a scramble for the knives, forks and spoons; then a greasy boy brought down a large dish containing roast beef and potatoes, and dumped it on the deck. The men clustered around the dish. One of them seized the meat with his left hand, hacked off a large piece with the dull knife in his right, clutched a handful of potatoes out of the dish, and then retired to a quiet corner with his prey. Each of the others did the same. When my turn came I had no appetite, and, until I left Southampton, my custom was to make up in town for my enforced abstinence aboard ship. The food was good in itself, and there was plenty of it, but it was wretchedly served, as I have mentioned. A bunk was assigned me, but I did not sleep much that first night. The next morning I went to Mr. Sawyer, the boatswain, and asked him for something to do. He proceeded to question me, found that I knew nothing of a sea-faring life, and told me very frankly that I was not worth my salt. However, he furnished me with a bucket and some soap, and told me to go to work and scour the paint. When I had amused myself with this for some hours, I was given a rag and told to polish up the brass-work. This ended, I occupied myself in sweeping decks and cleaning out spittoons. This was about the daily routine of my life on the *Nashville*. Usually only one man was on watch at night, and this part of the duty I found reasonably pleasant, as I could ensconce myself in the pilot house and read a novel to pass away the time, when I was not required on deck. The officers, especially the younger ones, were not particularly careful to return aboard at the appointed time, and I suppose that the dignified Solicitor of the Western Union Telegraph Company, Mr. Clarence Cary, has forgotten how I have connived at his slipping aboard, over the rail, when he had stayed in town longer than was good for him. Every day or two I was allowed to go ashore in the evening, and, leaving my sailor garb behind me, I led, for a few hours, a pleasant life in town. Mr. Sawyer, the boatswain, was very indignant one night, because he took off his hat and made me a profound bow, fancying that I was some distinguished visitor.

I think it was early in January, 1862, that a little commotion was caused by the report that the United States sloop-of-war *Tuscarora* had anchored in Southampton Water, and that Captain Craven, who was in command, had announced his intention to take the *Nashville* into either New York or Boston. Neither of these ports was our destination. Besides the eight seamen on the *Nashville*, we had about thirty firemen and coal-heavers, and in officers we were particularly rich, having, besides the Captain and Executive Officer, a Sailing-master, Purser, Doctor and seven Midshipmen. The men went ashore as often as they could obtain leave, or steal off unobserved, and the *Tuscarora's* men did the same.

There was a Music Hall at Southampton in those days, known as the "Rainbow" or the "Wheat Sheaf," which, being cheap and warm, was a favorite resort with us. The entertainment was not of a high order, but it answered the purpose. The sympathies of the Southampton people were unquestionably with the Confederates, and the *Tuscarora's* men were thought very little of. They had a hard time of it. When they went to the "Rainbow," any of the *Nashville's* men who happened to be there was sure to call out for the "Bonnie Blue Flag" or "Dixie," which was instantly played with the full force of the small orchestra, amid the hurrahs of the audience. But if the *Tuscarora's* men ventured to suggest "Yankee Doodle" or "Hail Columbia," they were hooted down incontinently. Consequently, fights were frequent, and, as the newspapers were friendly to us, the "Yankees" were always the aggressors, and were always the unfortunates to be locked up for the night, and lectured and fined by the magistrate in the morning. I must admit that we generally brought on the row ourselves, but, when it was over, and the wrong men had been put in the station house, we had the satisfaction of going down to the *Nashville*, singing lustily and giving cheer after cheer for the Southern Confederacy and Jeff Davis.

In the meantime, Captain Pegram had been in correspondence with the English Government, with regard to the threatening attitude of the *Tuscarora*, and it was announced officially that neither vessel would be allowed to leave Southampton within twenty-four hours after the departure of the other. This was kind, for, although there were many rumors concerning our armament, we really had but two guns, (12 pound Blakeley's) which had been lent to Captain Pegram by Governor Pickens, of South Carolina. Soon rumors came that we were about to sail in real earnest, and popular curiosity was so stimulated that crowds of persons came down from London to take a look at "the pirate." Many of them were disappointed at our peaceful appearance, but most of them agreed that the vessel was appropriately painted black. The *Nashville* was now hauled to the outer dock, and the authorities were notified that we were ready to sail. The appointed day was February 3, 1862, and thousands of persons, including many of our warm Southampton friends, thronged the docks. Amid cheers and waving handkerchiefs and cordial Godspeeds, the *Nashville*, at about half-past 3 o'clock in the afternoon, under a full head of steam, glided out into Southampton Water. Passing rapidly down the channel, the Confederate flag flying at the fore and mainmast, we saw lying off Osborne our old enemy, the *Tuscarora*, with steam up, but alongside was lying the British frigate *Shannon*, fully prepared to have a word to say, if Captain Craven should attempt to sail before the appointed time. This was some comfort to us, and we were soon gently rising and falling on the waves of the broad Atlantic.

I will give, at this place, some verses that I wrote at the time, and which used to be sung aboard. The air, as well as I remember, was very much like one that I had heard at the " Rainbow."

THE NASHVILLE DIXIE.

I.

'Tis long years since our fathers fought,
  Our Country dear to free ;
Our chartered rights, sealed with their blood,
  Were the fruits of victory.
They knew not how to cringe or kneel,
  The despot's train to swell,
The first deep thought in every breast
  Was to love old Dixie well.

CHORUS—Hurrah ! three cheers ! so gaily let us sing,
      Of all the lands that crown the earth
      Old Dixie's is the king.

2.

Our liberties are threatened now,
Armed hosts invade our soil.
Yet Northern bands, in hurried flight,
From Dixie's sons recoil.
We scorn their threats, deride their vows,
We know the foeman's worth,
No Vandal band shall e'er command
The land that gave us birth.

CHORUS—Hurrah! three cheers! so gaily let us sing,
Of all the lands that crown the earth
Old Dixie's is the king.

3.

The free-born rights our fathers won
Will we, their sons, maintain,
The honor of our spotless flag
Untarnished shall remain.
No Northern star shall ever shine
Where the Southern Cross has waved,
Nor while a hand can grasp a sword
Shall Dixie's be enslaved.

CHORUS—Hurrah! three cheers! so gaily let us sing,
Of all the lands that crown the earth,
Old Dixie's is the king.

III.

The morning after our departure from Southampton, the crew were mustered into the service of the Confederate States and signed the articles. I was rated as a "landsman," or a "boy." The crew were divided into two watches, and the regular routine of duty at sea began. I found that I had twelve hours on duty out of every twenty-four, and at no time more than four consecutive hours to call my own. For instance, to-day I would be on duty from 12 to 4 A. M., 8 A. M. to 12 M., 4 to 6 P. M., and 8 to 12 P. M., and so on in uninterrupted succession. This was rather hard work for one who was fond of comfort and late breakfasts, but I speedily learned not to lose any time in going to sleep, and undressing appeared a useless indulgence. This was not the worst of it. The wind was fair, and we had been running under the foresail, foretopsail and spanker, when some evil genius inspired the officer of the deck to order all hands aloft to reef the foretopsail. Now I knew nothing of gymnastics. I had never attempted to climb a greasy pole or a rope in my life, and was unaccustomed to any more difficult mode of reaching a given elevation than by the use of easy stairs, with a strong baluster. The *Nashville* was rolling handsomely, and I was not eager to respond to the call that had been made, hoping that my assistance would not be needed or expected by my hardy companions. But Sawyer, the boatswain, had no idea of allowing me to escape in that way, and enquired, in his usual polite way, whether I intended to be all day making up my mind. I told him I thought not, and started up the shrouds. Making a desperate effort to be lively, I missed every second or third ratline and scraped most of the skin off my shins. At last I reached the mast-head and got on the topsail yard. My calculation was that the best place for me was close to the mast, which I might hug with one arm while I helped to manipulate the flapping sail with the other; but the men who were up there would not hear of this. With much profanity, they told me that the proper place for me was out at the extreme end of the yard. Suspended under the yards, as customary, and parallel with it, was a foot rope. Planting my feet squarely against this, and resting my chest upon the yard and holding on like grim death with my hands, I got out to the yard-arm, but here the foot rope was so close to the yard that it was of little use to me. Just then one of the men gave the rope a jerk. My heels went up and my head went down, but I saved myself from falling by a violent effort and trusted the foot rope no more. Using both hands in lifting the sail, I balanced my body as well as I could upon the yard, and at this moment I confess I would not have given a sixpence for my chance of seeing the next morning's sun. I came down safe, however, as you perceive, and more scared than hurt. The men said that I left the marks of my fingers on the stays, and that the wood was indented where I grasped the yard. After a while I became accustomed to going aloft, although I never could make myself believe that it was better to be at the yard-arm than nearest the mast. The men were right, however, in regarding the former as the easiest berth, as the weight of the sail to be lifted is the least there.

The *Nashville* having been originally a passenger steamer, as I have already mentioned, carried only enough coal in the bunkers for six or eight days steaming, so we were soon employed in hoisting coal from the lower hold forward, and

3

running it aft to the bunkers. So long as the work was at the windlass on deck I got along very well, but, when I was sent down into the stifling atmosphere of the lower hold to fill the baskets with coal, I quickly ended the difficulty by fainting. When I revived, I went on deck and told Mr. Sawyer what had taken place. As one of the officers whom I knew was looking at him, he contented himself with saying that "I was no account anyhow, and might as well stay on deck."

This is as good a place as any to give the names of the officers: The commanding officer, as I said before, was Captain Robert B. Pegram, of Virginia; the First Lieutenant and Executive officer was Mr. Bennett; Lieutenant John J. Ingraham, of South Carolina, was the Sailing-master; the Second Lieutenant was Mr. Whittle, of Norfolk, Virginia; Dr. John L. Ancrum, of Charleston, was the Surgeon; Mr. Richard Taylor, of Norfolk, Virginia, was the Paymaster. The Midshipmen were: Thomas, of Georgia; McClintock, of Mississippi; J. W. Pegram (the Captain's son), of Virginia; Clarence Cary, of Virginia; Hamilton, of South Carolina; Sinclair, of Virginia; Dalton, of Mississippi. The Master-at-arms was Lewis Hill, of Richmond, Virginia. We had aboard, also, a Charleston pilot, Captain James Evans.

My intercourse with the officers was very pleasant while at Southampton, and I was on excellent terms with Cary, Pegram, Dalton, Hamilton and McClintock while we were at sea. They were careful, of course, not to allow their personal consideration for me to interfere in any way with a proper regard for the discipline of the ship. Cary was anxious to improve himself in French, and I gave him a lesson nearly every day. To one of the other midshipmen

I gave some lessons in music. The sailors were very much disgusted that any special kindness should be shown me, and really, until we reached Bermuda, this kindness on the part of the officers was confined necessarily to a friendly nod, or other greeting, excepting when I was giving any of the midshipmen such little assistance in French and music as I have mentioned.

The second day after we left Southampton my trunk was broken open and nearly everything I had in it was stolen by the sailors. I complained to Mr. Bennett, who suggested that I ought to have expected it, and should have been careful to keep my trunk securely locked, or to have had in it nothing that was worth stealing.

Captain Pegram did not appear to know that I was on board until we had been several days at sea. I was engaged one morning in sweeping the deck, or cleaning paint, when he stepped out from the pilot house, and seemed to recognize me. He nodded and said "good morning," and that was all. My heart sank and I felt forsaken.

IV.

In order to baffle the *Tuscarora*, who was sure to pursue us, Captain Pegram took a more northerly route than was usual; and on the fourth or fifth day after sailing the wind freshened sharply, and in a few hours blew with terrible force. The ship was old, and unprepared for bad weather, and it was not without anxiety that our officers saw the tempest approach. In twenty-four hours the gale had reached its height. The waves were running awfully high to my unaccustomed eyes, and were battering the sides of the ship as though determined to force an entrance. Nobly, however, did the *Nashville* behave. There surely never was a better sea boat. She shipped little water, and, although each wave that struck her bows made her tremble and quiver from stem to stern, she bore herself nobly in the unequal contest. Loose spars, boxes, coils of rope and water-casks, which had been improperly secured, were rolling about on deck, threatening to break the legs of whoever should pass. The port bulwarks from the heel of the bowsprit to the wheelhouse were washed away flush with the deck. One angry wave carried off the whole of the port wheelhouse and dashed to pieces several of the "buckets," or paddles. The saloon and the forward cabin were several inches deep in water, and the forecastle was in a worse plight. For days this continued. The engines were slowed down, and we did no more than hold our own. It would have been dangerous, lame as the vessel was, to drive her in the teeth of the tempest. The most grewsome part of it all was the unremitting tolling of the forecastle bell, as the *Nashville* rose on the crest of the wave and glided down, and down, into the trough of the sea.

THE BELL.

1.

A stormy night, the foaming waves,
In crested might, the good ship braves;
She seeks in vain the rest she craves,
Surging o'er dead seamen's graves,
While still is heard, o'er tempest's swell,
Thy low deep tones, O ! warning bell.

2.

The masts are gone, the timbers creak,
All work of mortal hands is weak ;
" Oh, God ! Oh, God ! she's sprung a leak,"
Each eye is dimmed and blanched each cheek,
And on each ear, a funeral knell,
Falls the note of the tolling bell.

3.

The boats are swamped ; in wild despair
Men cry aloud or bend in prayer ;
The poor ship groans, shrieks fill the air ;
A moment—and the ocean's bare.
But still is heard, as seamen tell,
When souls are lost, that warning bell.

While the gale was at its height the engine broke down, and sail was made to keep the vessel's head to the wind. The storm began to subside, and on the morning of the eighth day the wind had lulled. The waves still ran high, and for the first time I saw the beautiful effect of the dashing of the spray over the rail of the vessel, forming miniature rainbows arching to the deck and glowing and glittering with prismatic colors.

I suppose I ought to say at this point that I was very seasick on the first day out, but, as Bo'sun Sawyer was constantly after me to do some of the drudgery he had in mind for me, I had no time to indulge in the pleasures of sea-sickness and recovered entirely in less than twenty-four hours.

I had one very narrow escape during the gale. Crossing the hurricane deck, I was thrown off my feet by a sudden lurch of the vessel and went whirling to leeward. One of my feet caught in the rail as I was lurching overboard, and this was all that saved my Confederate career from being brought to an untimely end.

When the weather grew fine, the crew were ordered out for drill, and from the recesses of the hold our hidden armament was produced. It consisted of about twenty rusty smoothbore muskets. The muskets were given to the sailors and firemen, who were then drilled in the manual of arms by one of the officers. There was a good deal of difference of opinion as to what the commands meant, and the whole affair was very much of a burlesque, as every now and then a sudden lurch of the vessel would send three or four of the squad staggering down to leeward. When the command was given, Ready! Aim! and every musket was levelled at our instructor's head, the startled officer called out hastily: "For Heaven's sake, men, don't point your guns at me! They are loaded!" The warning was not given too soon, for, as they were dismissed, two of the men rolled into the scuppers, their pieces going off with a very ugly report. That was the first and the last of the drilling.

Although he had made no sign, Captain Pegram had not forgotten me. When we had been out seven or eight days, the Master-at-arms went to the boatswain and told him that I and a man named Lussen were to take one of the staterooms on the hurricane deck. This was paradise to me, for I had there every convenience that I required, and could escape from the loathsome company of the rest of the crew. Lussen was a singular character. He was evidently a thoroughly instructed sea-faring man and a good navigator. He had his sextant with him. According to his own account he had been an officer in the Navy of one of the South American Republics, and expected on reaching the Confederacy to get an appointment in the Confederate service. Being a very intelligent man, pleasing in his manners and not at all coarse, he was a welcome roommate and an acceptable companion. Our separation from the rest of the crew did not strengthen the men's kindly feeling for us, and they lost no opportunity of showing their spite and their disgust. One thing they insisted on, and that was that we should go down to the forecastle for our meals. A favorite dish once or twice a week was plum-duff, but the plums were so scarce that one of the men said that he could hear one plum singing this little song to another:

> Here am I! Where are you?
> Tell me where to find you.

In a letter that I wrote to my mother from Bermuda, I described our change of quarters as follows: "Our stateroom on the upper deck has two bunks and a toilet stand, and is very prettily painted. Through the windows we can look at the open sea. What a contrast to the den that we did inhabit! When work is over I can have the blessedness of being alone. More than this: one of the Midshipmen told me that he heard Captain Pegram and Mr. Bennett talking about me, and Captain Pegram said he was very much pleased with my conduct."

V.

On the evening of the 19th of February we were told that we might expect to make land the next morning, and as soon as the sun rose every one was on the lookout. In an hour or two land was in sight on the port bow, and even my unskilled eye could make out what seemed to be a long dark cloud on the horizon. Gradually the land became distinct, and by noon we were lying off Bermuda signaling for a pilot. The general aspect of the island was far from inviting, as nothing could be seen but rugged hills covered with dwarfed trees, and I looked in vain for the fine harbor of which I had heard so much. A boat with four negroes, who were making considerable fuss, came alongside with a splash, and, in great state, the black pilot clambered up the side and took his place in the pilot house. He understood his business. The *Nashville* ran squarely towards the island as though she was to be thrown upon the rocks. Then a narrow passage between two lofty hills was visible, and into this we steamed. Above our heads on each side towered the rocks, and the passage was so narrow that the yards seemed to scrape the trees on either side as we passed in. The passage gradually opened, and we dropped anchor in the beautiful harbor of St. George's. This harbor is, without exception, the most beautiful and picturesque that I have ever seen. There was not a ripple on the water, while dotting its brightly blue bosom in every direction were hundreds of islands, some of them of considerable size and others mere spots upon the placid surface of the harbor. The surrounding hills were adorned with houses built of white stone and shining like snow in the light of the sun. On the highest point was the signal station, where floated the red cross of St. George. It was near the end of February, yet the weather was warm and the sky was unclouded. It was hard to realize that only a few days before we had left cold fogs and drizzling rain in England.

The principal object in calling at Bermuda was to obtain a supply of coal, and Captain Pegram made a bargain with the master of a Yankee bark then in the harbor for as much as we needed. I think the coal had been intended to supply United States cruisers which were expected to stop at St. George's, but the high price we offered was too much for the patriotism of the master of the bark. I had a great desire to go ashore and see what Bermuda looked like, but this privilege was denied me as Bo'sun Sawyer found abundant occupation for the whole of us in shovelling coal and then scrubbing the paint. I was allowed on Sunday to be one of the boat's crew who went to the landing to bring off Captain Pegram, who had gone to church, and I had the satisfaction of waiting there in the sun for two or three hours and of being roundly abused, by the rest of the crew, for "catching crabs" in the most awkward manner as we rowed back to the *Nashville*.

Up to this time Captain Pegram had not determined positively whether he would run into Charleston, Savannah or New Orleans, and the information which he obtained at Bermuda satisfied him that these ports could only be reached with great difficulty, as the blockade had now become rigid. A ship captain whom he talked with informed Captain Pegram that he thought we might run into Beaufort, N. C., with comparative ease, and it was determined to try our fortune there.

After leaving Bermuda I was relieved from some of the

4

scrubbing and cleaning, and was allowed to take my turn as lookout, being posted for two hours at a time on the fore topsail yard. There I had the pleasantest hours that I knew on the *Nashville*. It was quiet and still. I was far removed from the bickering and blackguardism of the crew, and could indulge myself freely in watching the varied hues of the dancing waters, broken now and again by a shoal of porpoises, or by the brief flight of the flying-fish as they darted from the wave in the effort to escape from their pursuers. But all this was not conducive to keeping a sharp lookout. The second day after leaving Bermuda I was busily thinking of what might happen when we should reach our destination. The hail came from below: "Foretopsail yard there!"

I answered promptly "aye! aye! sir."

"Why haven't you reported that sail?"

I looked around the horizon and replied: "I have not seen a sail this morning, sir."

"No, I suppose not! come on deck!"

When I reached the deck I was received with a grin of derision, and found that a fine schooner was running under full sail within half a mile of us. I had looked too far. Every one too had been busy while I was dreaming aloft. The American flag was flying at our peak, and the men were now sent to the guns. A boat's crew was called away, and, eager to atone for my neglect, I jumped in. We pulled over to the schooner, which was now lying to, boarded her, and found her to be the *Robert Gilfillan*, from Boston to Hayti, with an assorted cargo. The master, a loquacious down-easter, was led to believe that the *Nashville* was the United States steamer *Keystone State*, and he invited the officer in charge of the boat to take breakfast with him.

The hot rolls looked most tempting, and the fragrance of the coffee was particularly tantalizing. The master, whose name was Gilfillan, told us that everything was going on splendidly for "the Union," and that the Union troops had been "whipping the bloody Rebels like forty." In fact, "the Rebellion was nearly played out." Lieutenant Ingraham, who was in command of the boat, very quietly said : "Haul down your flag and take your papers aboard my ship immediately."

"What for?" asked Captain Gilfillan.

The answer came promptly: "That vessel is the Confederate States steamer *Nashville*, and you are my prisoner."

The poor fellow was part-owner of the schooner, and I shall not soon forget the mingled dismay and astonishment on his face. But resistance was useless, and he did as he was ordered. All our boats were now lowered, and everything of value, the bells, chronometer, glasses and nautical instruments, some provisions, brooms and a lot of "notions," were taken aboard the *Nashville*. The schooner was then set on fire, and in a few hours had burned to the water's edge. For some days the hearts of the crew were gladdened by the fresh butter and choice Boston crackers which formed part of the stores of the ill-fated *Gilfillan*. The master and crew were given as comfortable quarters as we had, and all possible care was taken of them.

As we neared Beaufort every light was carefully covered at night, even the binnacle lamps being masked. At midnight we hove to for soundings, and found that we might expect to make land by daybreak. The men seemed to think that we should certainly be captured, and packed up their clothing in their bags ready for a run. No one slept much that night, and as soon as the fog lifted in the morn-

ing every eye was on the alert. Beaufort harbor was plainly
visible some miles distant, and we saw, besides, what we did
not care to see. "Sail astern!" shouted the lookout; and
then came the cry: "Sail on the starboard bow!" and then
again: "Sail on the port bow." Things looked rather blue.
The vessel astern did not cause us much anxiety, but the
blockaders on our port and starboard bows, although not
directly in our course, were so far ahead that if we attempted
to run in we might expect to be cut off. But Captain Pegram
was prepared for the emergency. "The Stars and Stripes"
were run up at the mainmast head, and a small private
signal of Messrs. Spofford & Tileston, the former agents of
the vessel, was run up at the foremast. Our course was then
changed so that we headed for the nearer of the two United
States vessels. The "Stars and Stripes" were displayed by
them, in response to our flags, and a vigorous signaling began. It was plain that the blockader could not make out
the meaning of Spofford & Tileston's pennant. On we went
without heeding this until Beaufort harbor was not more
than five or six miles distant on our starboard bow. We
could see the officers on the quarter-deck of the blockader,
and the men at the guns. The engines were slowed down,
and we blew off steam. The blockader nearest to us thought
that we had something to communicate, and lowered a boat.
As this was done, we hove round, the "Stars and Stripes"
came fluttering to the deck, and the Confederate flag was
run up at the foremast, the mainmast and the peak. With
all the steam we could carry, we dashed on towards Beaufort.
The Yankee now saw the trick, and fired a broadside at us.
No harm was done. She followed rapidly, firing occasionally from the bow guns; but without injury we
crossed the bar under the protection of the guns of

Fort Macon, and came safely to anchor near the railroad wharf, at Morehead City. For a little while we were in more danger from our friends than from the enemy. The commandant at Fort Macon took us for one of the enemy's vessels, and was about to open on us with his heavy guns, when one of his officers suggested that, as we were running towards the fort, they might as well wait until we were somewhat nearer. This proved our salvation. Before we had reached the point where they could effectively fire at us from the fort, we had shown our true colors and given the blockader the benefit of a clear pair of heels. It was a beautifully calm morning, and the *Nashville* surpassed herself. In splendid sailing trim and with little or no cargo, she must have made sixteen or eighteen knots as we ran into the harbor.

On the *Nashville* now all was joy, for the blockader attempted no further pursuit. The men hurrahed, and the officers tossed up their caps and congratulated each other on our success. Well they might. They were looking forward to a speedy reunion with their families and their friends. For the first time I realized my isolated position. There was no home or friends for me; nothing but doubt and uncertainty, yet I had confidence that with time, faith and energy, I might accomplish what I desired. The day, a pregnant one for me, was February 28, 1862.

VI.

Morehead City is not a large place. In fact, it consisted in 1862 of a railroad depot at the end of a long wharf. It was intended to be the great seaport of North Carolina, but, at this time, trade had refused to move out of its accustomed channel, and the only thing that gave the least shadow of animation to the place was the arrival and departure of the daily train with its few passengers for Beaufort, which lies across the Bay, a few miles distant. The railroad, which has its terminus at Morehead City, runs up to Goldsboro', where it connects with the main line of the Wilmington and Weldon Railroad. The *Nashville* was hauled alongside the wharf, and, as there was a faint expectation that the boats of the blockaders outside might come up at night and attempt to cut us out, preparations were made for a defence. The two Blakeley guns were placed on the wharf, and the muskets of which mention has been made before were brought up from the hold and prepared for use. The invaders, however, did not come, and there was nothing to disturb the solitude of the place but the occasional visit of gaunt North Carolina soldiers, attired for the most part in " butternut," otherwise homespun. They were in the Confederate service, and on duty in the neighborhood. Most of them were armed with flint-lock muskets or shot guns, and some of them carried huge bowie-knives made out of scythe blades. They were generally tall, sinewy fellows, and evidently accustomed to exertion and privation, but they were not the sort of troops that I had expected to find the Confederate army composed of. A group of them honored the *Nashville*, when she came in, with the true Confederate yell, which I then heard for the first time, and without admiring it.

As soon as I could obtain permission, I went up to Morehead City proper, if the Railroad station at the water's edge is not to pass by that name, and found there five or six wooden houses, a bar-room and the inevitable hotel. The clearing was small, and the pine woods came up to within a few yards of the hotel door. It was a barren country, and a joke among the sailors was that the hogs were so miserably poor that knots were tied in their tails by their prudent owners to keep them from slipping through the fences. Another story was that when a dog, in that part of North Carolina, found it necessary to bark, he leaned against a fence to keep from falling.

Captain Pegram went to Richmond to make his report, and took with him a number of mysterious boxes which had been brought aboard at Southampton. There was much speculation as to their contents, but I believe that they held nothing more dangerous than bank-note paper, postage stamps and lithographing apparatus. I remained aboard, of course, and there was little if any change in the routine of duty. There was paint to clean, and there were decks to sweep; the sails were to be unbent and sent below. I cannot say that my value as a sailor had increased materially during the voyage, and I had not even learned to tie, with any certainty, a fast knot. On the hurricane deck, as is usual on steamers, there was a score or two of wooden buckets for fire purposes. They were used occasionally for dipping up water. I tried my hand at it several times, while the vessel was in motion, and, when the bottom of the bucket was not driven out or the handle did not give way, I found, to my dismay, that I had made a

slippery hitch, and saw the bucket slip smoothly into the
water as soon as the strain came upon the line. Some of
the men made handsome buckets of canvas, which they
carefully embroidered, and I was not much more lucky
with these than I was with the wooden ones. I have mentioned how beautifully clear the water was in the harbor at
St. George's, Bermuda, and the time with me never seemed
to pass more slowly than when one of these fancy buckets
had escaped from my line and was settling down in the
water, and I had an agonizing expectation that Sawyer
would reach the spot where I was standing before it had
gone completely out of sight. I think that, at a moderate
calculation, I must be responsible to the Confederacy for
a dozen wooden buckets besides several canvas buckets.

It was now time that I should determine what to do.
The small newspaper published at Newbern, N. C., reached
us occasionally, and from this we received the first news of
the glorious victory of the *Virginia* in the fight at Hampton Roads, when she sank the *Cumberland* and the *Congress*.
There was great jubilation aboard that day. In the newspaper I found appeals for volunteers for different companies
then raising for the war. I cannot give a better idea of my
frame of mind than by saying that, at this time, I had determined to take my discharge from the *Nashville*, and de-
cide, by tossing-up, which one of the various companies
named in the newspaper I should join. I expected nothing better.

There was a surprise in store for me. One furiously cold
morning, immediately after the return of Captain Pegram
from Richmond, I was scraping the fore-yard, wet through
with the falling sleet and intensely uncomfortable, when one
of the boys from the ward-room came forward and called to

me to say that I was wanted in the saloon. I went below at once, and into the saloon, where I found Captain Pegram, who spoke very kindly, and told me that, when I first came aboard, he had thought that I was not serious in my avowed purposes, and that, for this reason, he had done nothing to encourage me; but that he and his officers had watched me very closely, and were so well pleased with my conduct that he had laid my case before the Secretary of the Navy, who had authorized him to appoint me a Master's Mate in the Confederate Navy. This announcement, so entirely unexpected, and which bridged for me, in a moment, the gulf which, aboard ship, separates the sailor from the officer, completely overwhelmed me. Captain Pegram saw my agitation, and told me that he should expect me to mess with him while we remained aboard, and that he would have my trunk placed in a state-room which he had ordered to be prepared for me. I went forward, thrust off my sailor's garb as rapidly as I could, put on the solitary civilian's suit which remained to me, and then was ready to receive the kind congratulations of the officers and the effusive demonstrations of regard of the truculent boatswain. Sawyer told me that he was delighted to hear of my promotion, which was just what he had expected, as he had always seen that I was not in the position that I ought to hold! Much to my regret I did not have the satisfaction of meeting Mr. Sawyer again after I left the *Nashville*, when I might have had the pleasure of telling him precisely what I thought of him and his ways. My only reply to his congratulations was to ask to be permitted to pay for the buckets I had disposed of in the ways I have described. He said it was of " no consequence."

5

VII.

What the precise position and duties of a Master's Mate were in the old navy I am not able to say. Indeed, I don't think I ever asked. In the Confederate Navy the Master's Mate had the same duties and the same nominal rank as a Midshipman, and wore the same uniform. The only difference was the very essential one that the pay of the Master's Mate was about $25 a month, while that of a Midshipman was about $40.

My worst troubles were now over. Captain Pegram told me that, as there was no special duty for me aboard, he would ask me to prepare, under his direction, his report of the voyage. This I did. It is worth remembering, too, that I had the pleasure of writing, in his name, a letter of thanks to Governor Pickens, of South Carolina, for the loan of the Blakeley guns which had constituted our armament. I remember that it was in this letter that Captain Pegram said that it was by means of these guns that the *Nashville* had been able to capture the *Harvey Birch* and the *Robert Gilfillan,* and had been able to show her teeth to the enemy. The last shot that we fired with these guns was at the block-aders as we ran into Beaufort. The shell fell short, but it was a sort of crow of defiance, and relieved our feelings somewhat.

I learned that the *Nashville* had been sold to a mercantile firm, and would be left at Morehead City in charge of two officers and three or four men, until the new owners should take possession of her. The rest of the crew were to be discharged, and the officers were to be sent to other posts of duty. I was ordered to report for duty to Commodore Forrest, at Norfolk, Va., to which point Captain Pegram was to go to take command of an iron-clad then building. To crown my satisfaction, Captain Pegram told me that he intended to make a visit to his family, in Sussex County, Virginia, and would be glad if I should accompany him, and remain with him until it was necessary to go to Norfolk.

On March 10, 1862, we bade good-bye to the *Nashville*. Shortly after our departure the enemy moved in force upon Newbern, and, to escape capture, Lieutenant Whittle and Midshipman Sinclair took the *Nashville* out to sea. They had but three or four men aboard, and were, I believe, without charts or chronometers. They ran down to Charleston, and being unable to get into that port, went to Savannah, where they succeeded in running the blockade. It was a daring feat most successfully accomplished, and reflected the highest credit on the officers and men. The *Nashville* lay in the Ogeechee river until 1863, when she was named the *Rattlesnake*, and was made ready for sea as one of the vessels of the Volunteer Navy then forming. But a Federal gunboat succeeded in setting her on fire with shells thrown across the marsh to the point where she lay, and she burned to the water's edge and sank. This was the end of as fine a sea-boat as was ever built.

On taking the train to Goldsboro' I found that the passport system was in full operation, and, as I was in civilian's dress, the guard declined to allow me to pass. Captain Pegram, however, told the guard that he would "endorse" me, and I went on without molestation. Of course I made all manner of queer blunders. Everything was so strange. The nocturnal noise of the tree frogs caused me to tell Captain Pegram in the morning that it was the only country that I had ever been in where the birds sang all night. I had not then been kept awake, hour by hour, by the melodious warbling of the mocking bird.

It was a little after daylight when we reached Stony Creek, on the Petersburg and Weldon Railroad, where we were to leave the train. Taking a carriage after breakfast, we drove through the woods and plantations to the residence of Major Belsches, with whom Captain Pegram's family were staying. Two or three miles before reaching it, we passed by a handsome residence in the midst of a large and well-ordered plantation, which I was told belonged to Mr. Nat. Raines, a wealthy planter, who was an old friend of Captain Pegram's. At the house of Major Belsches we found Mrs. Pegram, her two daughters and her two younger sons. Every one was as kind as possible, and the time for our departure for Norfolk came far too soon. Before going there—indeed, the very day after our arrival—I was taken over to the residence of Mr. Raines, to be introduced to him and his family. He seemed to take quite a fancy to me, and in the course of a few hours I was on a friendly footing with the whole family. Nat. Raines, Jr., and Dr. B. F. Raines, the sons of Mr. Raines, were in the cavalry service, and, at this time, at home on furlough. Mrs. Raines was quiet, gentle and motherly, and her two daughters I found to be amiable and accomplished. One joke that Mr. Raines had was to tell me that he was fonder of smoking than I, and could out-smoke me. The tournament that followed resulted in my ignominious defeat. The weapons were Powhatan clay pipes with long reed stems, charged with tobacco grown on the plantation. Mr. Raines carried a supply of it usually in his coat pocket.

VIII.

Arrived at Norfolk, I reported to Commodore Forrest, and was ordered by him to go aboard the *Confederate States*, the receiving ship. This was a line-of-battle ship, named formerly the *United States*, which had escaped destruction by the Federals upon their evacuation of the navy yard. On the receiving ship, where there were a number of officers awaiting orders, I had my first experience of a hammock. Like one of the heroes of my favorite Marryatt, I signalized my entrance into the hammock on one side by pitching out on my head on the other side. Unlike Marryatt's heroes, however, no shot-box with a sharp edge had been kindly placed on the deck, by a sympathizing mess-mate, to meet my descending skull. Having little to do aboard, I made the acquaintance of Captain James Barron Hope, who was acting as Commodore Forrest's Secretary, and assisted him in the discharge of his pleasant duties. Captain Hope is widely known as a writer of both fervent verse and delightful prose. He has been for some years the proprietor and editor of the Norfolk *Landmark*, which is published at Norfolk, where he lives. His latest literary work is the noble Centennial Ode which was read last year at the celebration at Yorktown.

Having provided myself with the gray uniform of the Confederate Navy, I was taken to see Commodore Franklin Buchanan, who commanded the *Virginia* in her first fight, when he was severely wounded. The *Virginia* was in dock, and was being put in order for another cruise; and Commodore Buchanan was deeply chagrined at the prospect that she might be ready before he had recovered. On March 25

Commodore Josiah Tatnall was placed in command of the squadron at Norfolk.

Much has been written about the *Virginia*, but those who saw her will agree, I think, that it was marvellous that she should have accomplished what she did. The plating consisted of railroad iron rolled flat, and the bends were protected by iron knuckles. There was no plating below the water-line, and the prow with which she did so much execution did not look much more dangerous than a champagne bottle, which, in shape, it resembled. The great defect of the *Virginia*, however, was the weakness of her engines, which prevented her from manœuvering rapidly, and which placed her at so terrible a disadvantage in the fight with the Monitor. The engines broke down frequently while she was in the United States service. Their peculiar construction, taken in connection with the great draft of the vessel, twenty-two feet, and her length, three hundred and twelve feet, rendered her management in narrow channels and in presence of the enemy a very difficult matter.

The Confederate fleet at Norfolk consisted of the *Virginia*, eight guns; the *Patrick Henry*, eight guns; the *Jamestown*, two guns; and the *Beaufort*, the *Raleigh* and the *Teaser*, one gun each. The *Patrick Henry* and *Jamestown* were ordinary river steamboats, hastily and rudely adapted to the reception of heavy guns; while the *Raleigh*, the *Beaufort* and the *Teaser* were small and weak tug-boats. An ordinary rifle ball would have perforated the boiler of the war-tugs, and a shell from a field-piece, if it hit at all, would be tolerably sure to send any one of them to the bottom. With this fleet, however, it was determined to attack the Monitor and the other United States vessels of war near Fortress Monroe. I volunteered for service in the fleet, and was assigned to duty on the *Beaufort*, which was commanded by Lieutenant W. H. Parker, one of the finest officers in the Navy. Picked men from the infantry regiments stationed at Norfolk were placed on each of the vessels; and, the *Virginia* now being in tolerable order again, the whole fleet, on the morning of April 11, 1862, steamed past Norfolk, and gaily down the river, the *Virginia* leading the line. The wharves along the river were crowded with ladies and soldiers. Hats were tossed in the air, handkerchiefs were waved, and cheer after cheer rent the air. The enthusiasm of the hour made every one feel like a hero. Captain Parker told me that the main object of the expedition was the capture and destruction of the Monitor. Commodore Tatnall was desperately in earnest, and one of the midshipmen of the *Virginia* told me that he heard the old Commodore say, as he stumped up and down the quarter-deck, gritting his teeth: "I will take her! I will take her! if h—ll's on the other side of her." The "her" was understood to be the Monitor. The plan of operations was bold and simple. When the Monitor came out to meet us, the *Patrick Henry*, the *Jamestown*, the *Beaufort* and the *Raleigh*, at a signal from the *Virginia*, were to run down upon the enemy, endeavoring to strike her on the bows and quarter. The Monitor was to be mobbed by the gun-boats while the *Virginia* engaged her attention. On each of the Confederate vessels boarding parties were detailed with prescribed duties. Those numbered one in each vessel were provided with hammers and wedges, and were to endeavor to chock the turret of the Monitor so as to prevent it from revolving, in which case her line of fire could only be changed by moving the vessel. Those numbered two were supplied with balls of tow, steeped in turpentine, which were to be ignited and

thrown down the ventilators, which were then to be covered.
Those numbered three were to throw a wet sail over the pilot-
house so as to blind the helmsman.   Meanwhile other boarders, armed with pistols and cutlasses, were to guard against
any attempt on the part of the enemy's crew to escape
from the confinement which was prepared for them.   I had
command of the boarders on the *Beaufort*.   The general
idea was that the Monitor would be overwhelmed by the
combined attack; and that by the means indicated we
could prevent her from doing much harm.   The *Virginia*
would play an important part by endeavoring to ram her,
and we hoped to be able, with our four boarding steamers,
to take the Monitor in tow and haul her back to Norfolk,
when we might break her open, and take the crew prisoners
at our leisure.   Commodore Tatnall expected that probably
half his gun-boats would be sunk or crippled in the attempt,
but he was quite sure of throwing on the deck of the Monitor men enough to ensure her capture.   It is just as likely
that the Monitor would have towed us to Fortress Monroe,
if she had not sunk the whole concern before we reached
her.   The weather was dirty, and we lay at anchor during
the night off Craney Island.   Betimes the next morning we
dropped down to Hampton Roads.   The enemy's batteries
fired several shots at us without effect.   We could see that
the Monitor had steam up, and was lying close under the
protection of the batteries.   She looked like a huge black
plate with a cheese box of the same color upon it.   The
flag ship *Minnesota*, with a large number of men-of-war and
merchantmen, was below the forts.   Signal guns were fired,
and we hoped that the enemy would engage us.   The day
wore on and still the Monitor and her consorts skulked
under the guns of the forts.   The *Virginia* ran within range

of the formidable fortress, and then fired a gun of defiance, but the Monitor would not come to the scratch. Within the bar at Hampton three merchant vessels were lying, and the *Jamestown* and *Raleigh* ran in, captured them and brought them out. This exploit, almost within gunshot of the Monitor, did not affect her movements. We did not get the fight we sought. It was a terrible disappointment. But in the critical condition in which the United States Navy was at the time, it was the wiser part for the Monitor to decline the engagement. Had we succeeded in disabling her, the whole coast would have been at the mercy of the *Virginia*. Obstructions had already been placed in the Potomac in expectation of a naval raid on Washington, and there was considerable perturbation at New York and Boston.

6

IX.

On April the 17th I received orders to proceed to Petersburg, and join Captain Pegram there. The iron-clad which was building at Norfolk was not likely to be ready for several months; and, as Captain Pegram was anxious to be in active service, he was assigned to the command of the iron-clad *Louisiana*, which was building at New Orleans, and said to be nearly finished. With his usual kindness he caused me to be ordered to the same vessel, and asked me to go down with him. My first visit to the "Cockade City" was a very agreeable one, as I made acquaintance there with a number of Captain Pegram's relatives, including his niece, Mrs. Annie T. White, and his sister, Mrs. David May.

From Petersburg the journey by railroad to Louisiana was dreary and monotonous in the extreme. I have a bare recollection of being invited at Kingville, S. C., to go to the end of the station and inspect an astonishingly fat hog, which was the wonder of that part of the country. There really was no other incident of note that I recall, except the frequent delays, and the arrival at different points too late for the connecting trains. As we neared our destination, the air was full of ugly rumors. We learned that the United States fleet had attacked the forts below New Orleans, and it was reported that the city had been evacuated. But we pressed on, and finally reached Jackson, Miss., where we were told that it was no use to go any further. No passenger trains were now running, but we succeeded in getting on a train that was going down, and got within twenty miles of New Orleans. There the cars were stopped; and in a short time train after train came up from the city, bringing out the Confederate troops, under command of General Mansfield Lovell, and such stores as could be carried off. A number of the soldiers who belonged to the " Garde d'Orleans," flatly refused to go any further, and, to my surprise, were allowed to return to the city, which was now in the possession of Butler's forces. There was no choice for us but to go back to Virginia ; and Captain Pegram took charge of dispatches from General Lovell, giving an account of the disaster. So it turned out that, by stopping a day or two at Petersburg, we had missed an opportunity of participating in one of the fiercest naval fights of the war. The vessel which Captain Pegram was to have commanded was taken down the river in an unfinished condition, and was either sunk or was blown up. The journey back was worse than the journey down, as the delays were multiplied. It was on the train, soon after leaving Lovell's troops at Tangipahoa, that I first met Colonel James M. Morgan (then a midshipman), whose sister I afterwards married. The vessel on which he was serving, the *McRae*, was lost in the engagement, and he made his escape from the city with great difficulty.

When we reached North Carolina there was no comfort there. Norfolk had been evacuated by the Confederate forces, and the *Virginia* had been destroyed to prevent her from falling into the hands of the enemy. I received permission to rest in Sussex for a few days, and then went to Richmond, where I was assigned to duty on a floating battery lying in the James River, and commanded by Captain Parker, with whom I had served on the *Beaufort*. This so-called battery was a large flat, with a shield heavily plated with iron in front. The name of the battery was the *Drewry*, and she lay at Rockett's, below Richmond. I had fancied that she was a vessel of the same class as the *Vir-*

11

ginia, and when I went down to the place where she lay I
looked about vainly for the vessel.   Hailing a man who was
at work on what I supposed to be a dredge, I asked which
was the *Drewry*.   "This is she," said he.   I was both disappointed and disgusted.   The *Drewry* was really a lighter,
about eighty feet long and fifteen feet broad, and was intended to be loaded down within eight or ten inches of the
water.   She had a wooden shield, V shaped, covered with
heavy iron bars, and in the angle of the shield was cut a
port-hole for her one heavy gun.   She had no engines or
sails, and was to be towed or allowed to drift into position
when an engagement was expected.

I engaged quarters at a very pleasant house in Franklin
Street, and found amongst the boarders there the mother
and sister of Clarence Cary, whom I had known on the
Nashville.   The sister, Miss Constance Cary, married, after
the war, Mr. Burton N. Harrison, who was the private secretary of President Davis.   Miss Constance Cary, or Miss
"Connie," as she was usually called, wrote a good deal in
war times under the *nom de plume* of "Refugitta;" and
during the last few years has written at least one very
charming society novel, besides an admirable work on
household decoration.   There were also there, in the pleasant company, Miss Hettie Cary, the famous Baltimore
beauty, and her sister, Miss Jennie Cary, a handsome woman, and unfailingly amiable.   Of course she was overshad-
owed by her sister; and she used to say that the only
inscription necessary for her tomb-stone would be: "Here
lies the sister of Hetty Cary, the lady who presented
the Confederate colors to Beauregard's troops at Manassas."
Miss Hetty Cary, late in the war, married General John W.
Pegram, a nephew of Captain R. B. Pegram.   A fight took

place two or three weeks after her marriage, and Mrs. Pegram went immediately to the front to assist in caring for the wounded. Almost the first man who was brought up, as she reached the field hospital, was her dead husband. The Carys and Captain Pegram's sister-in-law, Mrs. General Pegram, and her daughters, Miss Mary and Miss Virginia Pegram, were as kind and considerate to me as if I had been a member of their family. To one of Captain Pegram's nephews, Willie Pegram, the youngest son of Mrs. General Pegram, I became very warmly attached. He was at this time particularly boyish looking, and wore spectacles, which added to the simplicity of his appearance. A graduate of the Virginia Military Institute, he had gone into service as a private in Company F of the First Virginia Regiment, and upon the promotion of Captain Lindsey Walker, had been elected Captain of the Purcell Battery.

My time in Richmond passed almost too pleasantly. I was not satisfied with myself, and saw no prospect of accomplishing anything as long as I remained in the Navy. McClellan's army was close to Richmond, and one fine morning, at the end of May, the battle of Seven Pines began. I obtained leave of absence, and, armed with a navy sword, hastened down to the field, arriving there about night-fall. The first troops I fell in with at the front belonged to a Georgia regiment, the Eighth Georgia, I think; and I asked to be permitted to take a musket and go in with them as a volunteer, the next morning. Next morning came, but the fight did not, and I trudged disconsolately back to Richmond.

I now made up my mind to leave the Navy. Fearing that Captain Pegram would object to this, I went to the Navy Department myself and handed in my resignation, which had been approved by Captain Parker.   I took care to say that I only resigned in order that I might go into the army as a private soldier.   My purpose was to join the Purcell Battery, which Willie Pegram commanded, but he refused to consent to this, telling me that if I waited something better would turn up.   I was not willing to wait, and went out to the battery and reported to him for duty a few days before the Seven Days Battle began.

X.

The camp of the Purcell Battery was then on the Mechanicsville Turnpike, as well as I remember; and it was a
day or two after my arrival that the Confederate battle
flags were first distributed to the Army of Northern Virginia.   I remember, as though it were yesterday, the return
of Willie Pegram from head-quarters, with the battle flag
for our battery.   It was only a square of coarse cloth with
a blue field and a red cross dotted with stars.   But to the
soldiers of the Confederate armies it was then the emblem
of all that we fought for, as it is now the token of what the
Confederate soldiers endured, and of what our people lost.

At the time of the battles around Richmond the Artillery
had not been formed into battalions, as was done later in
the war; and to each brigade was attached one field-bat-
tery.   The Purcell Battery was attached to Field's Brigade,
of A. P. Hill's Division.

Early in the afternoon of Thursday, June 26th, 1862, the
head of General Hill's column crossed the Chickahominy,
and moved towards Mechanicsville.   It was the first time I
had seen the Confederate troops marching to meet the
enemy; and the gleaming bayonets, and waving flags, the
rumbling of the artillery, and the steady tramp of the men,
were both exhilarating and imposing.   One of Field's regiments led the advance, with two guns from our battery.
We neared a narrow road between two steep banks, and
were confident that we should feel the enemy there.   There
was a puff of smoke and the sharp crack of a rifle; the skirmishers advanced, and we threw some shells into the woods.
The skirmishers kept steadily forward.   They entered the

woods and were lost to sight. Soon they reached the
enemy's line, and the engagement began. We had now
reached a point near Ellyson's Mill, at Mechanicsville, which
had been strongly fortified by the enemy. They had a battery in position, and amused themselves by taking pot-shots
at us. Willie Pegram, however, remained motionless in his
saddle, no more concerned at the shells which were plough-
ing up the dust about him than if he had been lounging on
the porch in Franklin Street, this beautiful evening. An
officer rode hurriedly up, and then the order rang out:
" Attention, Battery! Forward! Trot! March!" and with
a cheer we rattled along the road and came into battery in
an open field, in full view of the enemy. The guns were
instantly loaded, and the firing began. The Yankees were
not idle; and a shower of shot and shell enveloped us. I
had not been assigned, as yet, to any particular duty in the
battery, and looked on as an interested observer until accident should make a vacancy that I might fill. I tied my
horse behind a corn crib, near by, and awaited developments,
walking up and down in the rear of the guns to see what
was going on. It was not an agreeable situation, as there
was nothing to divert my attention from the manifold un-
pleasantnesses of the terrific fire which the enemy concen-
trated upon us. They had twenty-four guns in position
against our single battery, and were able to enfilade our
line, as well as to pound us by their direct fire. It was
one of the greatest errors of the early days of the Confederacy that batteries were allowed to be knocked to pieces
in detail, when, by massing a dozen batteries, the enemy
could have been knocked quickly out of time and many
lives saved. A solid shot bowled past me, killed one of our
men, tore a leg and arm from another, and threw three

horses into a bloody, struggling heap.   This was my chance, and I stepped to the gun and worked away as though existence depended on my labors.   For the great part of the time I acted as Number 5, bringing the ammunition from the limber to Number 2 at the piece.   I felt for the first time the fierce excitement of battle.   There was no thought of danger, though the men were falling rapidly on every side.

So the battle continued until about six o'clock, the men cheering wildly whenever there was any sign of weakening on the part of the enemy.   I did not know what hurt me; but I found myself on the ground, hearing, as I fell, a man near me say: "That Britisher has gone up at last."   In a few moments I recovered my senses, and found that I was not dead, and that no bones appeared to be broken.   The warm blood was pouring down my left leg, and on examination I saw that a piece of shell had scooped out five or six inches of the flesh below the knee, and near the femoral artery, making an ugly wound.   I did not feel that I was disabled, however, and, tying a handkerchief as tightly as I could around my leg, I went back to my post, and there remained until the battery was withdrawn after sunset. Towards the end of the engagement only three men were left at the gun at which I was serving.   At a second gun only four men were left.   Another battery relieved us, and drew some of the enemy's fire.   But I think it must have been nine o'clock when we finally left the field.   The official list of casualties in our battery showed four killed and forty-three wounded, out of about seventy-five who went into the engagement.   Among the killed was Lieutenant Elphinstone.

The battle-field was several miles from Richmond, and the problem was, how to get back there.   I hobbled a part

7

of the way as well as I could, and was then put into an
ambulance with two wounded men, one of whom died
before we reached Richmond. I stopped at a Field Hospital for a minute to get some morphine for my wounded
comrade, and then had my first experience of scientific
butchering. A rough table, consisting of two or ·three
planks, was used for the operations; and there the surgeons
were hard at work, their sleeves rolled up to the shoulders,
their arms and hands besmeared with blood, cutting deep
with their knives into the quivering flesh, or sawing with a
harsh grating sound through the bones of the insensible
soldier. Under the table lay arms, hands, feet, and legs,
thrown promiscuously in a heap, like the refuse of a slaughter house.

XI.

Upon reaching Richmond I was taken to my old quarters in Franklin Street, and made much of. The Richmond *Dispatch*, after describing the battle in which we had been engaged and giving a list of the casualties in our battery, said: "This list proves the desperate bravery exhibited by the command in the bloody strife. We learn that Mr. Dawson, a young Englishman, who came over in the *Nashville*, volunteered for the engagement, and received a wound while acting most gallantly." My old friends in the Navy (and the Navy officers are more clannish and stick together more closely than the Army officers do,) came at once to see me. First, of course, was my dear friend, Captain R. B. Pegram, who chided me for resigning from the Navy without telling him what I was going to do. Commodore Hollins, Commodore Forrest, and Captain Arthur Sinclair, were exceedingly attentive. The surgeons told me there was no danger of serious results from my wound, if severe inflammation could be prevented; and Captain W. H. Murray, of one of the Maryland regiments, rigged up an arrangement for me by which water was allowed to drip, night and day, on the bandages, to keep them moist and cool. Miss Hetty Cary rather turned the tables on me, by sending me word that she would have come down to my room with her sister to see me, but that I had criticised so sharply, before I had been hit, the conduct of ladies who had gone to the hospitals to attend to the wounded soldiers, that she would not think of doing violence to my feelings now by giving me any of her personal attention. In truth, the young ladies who did visit hospitals were disposed to be rather partial in their attentions. There were pet patients wherever the young ladies were allowed to go. A very good illustration is given in a paragraph which went the rounds of the Southern papers, as showing the experience of an interesting wounded soldier, who had dark eyes and a darling mustache, and a generally romantic aspect. A young lady said to him: "Is there not anything that I can do for you?" Wearily the soldier said: "Nothing, I thank you." Not to be baffled, the young lady said: "Do let me do something for you. Will you let me wash your face for you?" The sad response of the soldier was: "Well, if you want to right bad, I reckon you must; but that will make seven times that my face has been washed this evening." There were some patriotic verses on the same subject, written in all seriousness, which ended with this touching couplet:

> "And every day there is a rush
> To give the soldiers milk and mush."

The doctors complained, too, that the young ladies were rather in their way; and that their prescriptions were oftentimes set at nought by surreptitious doses of pies and sweetmeats. But the motive was always good and pure, and, after I had known what it was to be hit myself and to need a woman's attentions, I was not disposed to quarrel with any one, however fascinating, for being assiduous in attentions to a wounded Confederate.

As soon as I was able to stand up, Captain Murray offered to go with me to Petersburg, where I might remain until I recovered. Mrs. Annie T. White invited me to stay at her house, and I was there for several weeks. While there, Mr. John Dunlop, who has been one of the staunchest friends I have had, called to see me. He was a native of Peters-

burg, but was educated in England, and took the degree of
A. M. at Wadham College, Oxford, not long before the
beginning of the war.   He went to New York to practice
law there ; but returned to Virginia as soon as the State
seceded, and joined one of the Virginia regiments as a
private.   He was appointed aide-de-camp to General Armistead, which was the position he held at the time ·that I
first knew him.   After the second battle of Manassas he
was retired on account of his failing sight, and went to
England.   After the war he returned to Virginia, and is
now living at Richmond, where he pursues his profession ·
with much success.

Murray returned to Richmond in a day or two.   Poor
fellow ! I never saw him again.   He was killed at Gettysburg.   I have fancied that he was deeply attached to Miss
Jennie Cary, who has never married.

Mr. Raines was greatly concerned at hearing that I had
been wounded, and sent his carriage to Petersburg to take
me down to his house in Sussex.   He told me that his
house must be my home.   In his own simple and heartfelt
language : " My dollars and cents I will divide with you ;
and half my bread and meat is yours."

As soon as I was able, I went from Petersburg to Sussex,
and there remained until I had recovered completely.   It
was here, at Oakland, as the plantation of Mr. Raines was
named, that I learned what Southern life really was.   I
was treated in every respect as one of the family, and was
hailed by the darkies, big and little, as part of the establishment.   They did, however, have a rather unpleasant
way of prognosticating an untimely end for me, as I heard
the little negroes chanting continually : " Poor Mas'r Frank !
he bin sure to die long before de acorn come."

Captain Robert B. Pegram was staying at the place of Major Belsches, about two miles away, and one morning Nat. Raines, Jr., and I drove over to make him a visit. As we passed by the mill, about half way, we met Captain Pegram in a buggy, and saw that his benignant face was shining even more brightly than usual. His first words were: " Dawson, I have some good news for you." I asked him what it was, and he handed me a note from his cousin, Mrs. G. W. Randolph, the wife of the Secretary of War. The words were few, but they were pregnant words for me. They were these:

" DEAR COUSIN ROBERT:

Mr. Randolph has ordered a commission as First Lieutenant of Artillery to be made out for Mr. Dawson.

Yours, sincerely,

MARY RANDOLPH."

The cup of my happiness was full. Standing in the streets in Richmond, and watching the troops as they passed, I had so often wondered whether, in the course of time, I might hold a commission in the Confederate army; and now it had come to me unexpectedly, unsolicited, undeserved. I learned afterwards that Willie Pegram had been so good as to recommend my appointment on account of my behavior at Mechanicsville; and his recommendation was vigorously sustained by his uncle, Captain Robert B. Pegram, and my Navy friends. The Confederate government had no power to appoint company officers for the volunteer forces; and for this reason I did not receive a commission in the line. My appointment was under an Act of the Confederate Congress, which authorized the appointment of forty First Lieutenants of Artillery for assignment to duty as Ordnance officers.

XII.

There was joy indeed at Oakland when the news of my promotion was received there; and the young ladies set themselves to work at once to contrive ways and means whereby my gray Navy coat could be converted into the tunic of an Artillery officer. The most troublesome part of it all, we found, was to get the Austrian knot on the arm, the "curleyqueue," as we called it, into the right shape. It is so long since, and these things are so soon forgotten, that it may not be out of place to mention here that my new uniform was a gray tunic with scarlet cuffs and scarlet collar; an Austrian knot of gold braid on each arm; two bars of gold lace, denoting the rank, on each side of the standing collar; gray trousers with broad red stripes; a scarlet kepi, trimmed with gold braid, and commonly known, by the way, as the "woodpecker cap."

One important consideration for me about this time was, how I should get the money to pay for a horse and other necessary equipments. Mr. Raines had two sons in the service, and was, as I knew, supporting the families of several soldiers from the neighborhood. He came to me, however, and told me that he had instructed his factors at Petersburg, to honor any drafts that I might make upon them; and that I must go there and get the money necessary for a horse, and anything else that I wanted. This was more than I was willing to accept; but I had not much choice in the matter; and Mr. Raines assured me that it was a pleasure to him to be able to assist me in preparing myself to fill properly the position that I had won. So off I went to Petersburg, and thence to Richmond, in all the brilliancy of gray and scarlet and gold ; the little darkies on the plantation, as I drove off from Oakland, singing the refrain that I have mentioned before.

I had not yet been assigned to duty with any particular command, and had not the remotest idea of what kind of duty it was to be ; but I had heard a good deal of General Longstreet, and when I reached Richmond, I went to the Ordnance Bureau to have a preparatory talk with Colonel Gorgas, who was Chief of Ordnance of the army. I began to realize, from what I saw around me, that I was likely to be in a worse plight as an Ordnance officer, whatever that might be, than I was as an able bodied seaman, so-called, on the *Nashville ;* and I said frankly to Colonel Gorgas, that I felt inclined to decline the commission which had been tendered me. He asked me why I intended to take such a step. I said that I knew nothing whatever of the duties of an Ordnance officer, and hardly knew the difference between a Napoleon gun and a Belgian rifle. I did not think it right, therefore, to undertake what I did not think I would be able to perform satisfactorily. Colonel Gorgas looked at me a moment to see whether I was in earnest or not, and then said very quietly : " I think you had better accept the commission ; I reckon you know as much about it as many other officers who have been assigned to the same duty." I took him at his word, and asked to be assigned to General Longstreet's corps. At the same time I mentioned to Colonel Gorgas that I did not want any duty in the rear ; and he gave me a letter to General Longstreet, requesting that, if any particularly hazardous service should fall within the line of my duty, it might be given to me.

It was difficult to get such a horse as I wanted in Richmond; but I succeeded in getting a respectable iron sabre with a painted scabbard, and I bought a good revolver and an imitation McClellan saddle. With these, and a large valise as my baggage, I went down to the Virginia Central Railroad station to take the train for Culpepper C. H., which was the nearest point on the railroad to the place where the army was believed to be. I should mention that, after the battles around Richmond, Jackson had attacked and defeated the enemy at Cedar Mountain; and the whole army of Northern Virginia was now in motion towards Manassas. I met, at the station, Captain Taylor, of Norfolk, a naval officer, who had been appointed Captain of artillery, and assigned to duty with Stephen D. Lee's battalion of reserve artillery. We traveled together, and left the cars at Culpepper C. H. By dint of hard talking, we obtained quarters for the night at the hotel, and the next morning we set out to overtake the army. I left my valise with the hotel-keeper; but I could not consent to part with my saddle, which I lugged along as best I could.

8

XIII.

The roads were sandy and the day was intensely hot, and the weight of the saddle increased every mile. Soon we struck a column of troops marching in the same direction as ourselves, and the men began the usual chaff. " I say, Mister," said one, "who stole your horse?" Another, in an expostulatory tone of voice, rejoined: " Why don't you let him alone; don't you see that the other man is going to get up and ride?" Then again: " Come out of that saddle; it's no use to say you ain't there; I can see your legs sticking out." One man very demurely stepped up to Captain Taylor, and said: "You must not mind these boys, sir; they don't mean any harm by it." He replied very courteously: " I don't mind it all, my friend." " Well," continued the man, " they don't mean any harm, but they always carry on in that way whenever they see a d—d fool come along." This last sally caused a shout all along the line; and we were glad enough to part company with them.

That night we met with some of Captain Taylor's friends, who gave us supper; after which we had a bath in a creek near by, and, rolled up in our blankets, had an excellent sleep.

In the morning we were on the road betimes; and I managed to stow away my saddle in a wagon. There were all manner of rumors concerning the whereabouts of Longstreet, and we kept on until we reached the little village of Stevensburg. No positive information could be obtained here; but we found a man who was willing to let us have dinner. We enjoyed the meal thoroughly, chatting merrily the while. Two or three citizens came into the room and scrutinized us closely, but we paid no attention to them. Presently, after whispering among themselves, one of them approached me and said: "What battery do you belong to, sir?" "None at all," I replied; and went on with my dinner. Shortly he returned, and said: "What State do you hail from, sir?" "None at all," I replied, "except a state of semi-starvation." This seemed to annoy him, and he tried me once more: "Where are you going to?" "To General Longstreet's head-quarters," I answered. "What for, sir?" questioned the stranger. In the meanwhile I had finished my dinner, and feeling very comfortable, I turned to Captain Taylor and said: "I have heard a great deal of the curiosity of Americans, and I am disposed to gratify it as far as I can conveniently; but this man is becoming a bore." The inquiring citizens now took a new turn, and asked Captain Taylor where he was going to. Whereupon he told them that it was none of their business. We paid our bill, and got up to leave the room, when one of the citizens quietly closed the door, and said: "Men, you, can't leave here until you show your papers!" "The devil we can't!" said I. "What right have you to ask for our papers?" The answer came sharply enough: "We ask for your papers by the right that every true citizen has to question men whom he suspects to be deserters or worse." Both Captain Taylor and I were rather high tempered. I had a great idea of my own dignity as a Confederate officer, and I told our inquiring friends at once that we positively refused to show any papers or answer any more questions. They told us that they would not allow us to depart until we did. Captain Taylor drew his pistol, and I drew my Confederate-iron sabre, and a lively fight of two to four was imminent. At this moment there was a violent knocking at the door, and a cavalry officer with two or three dismounted cavalrymen, came in. The citizens took him out and talked with him; and when they returned the officer asked us where we wanted to go to. Captain Taylor said he wanted to find General Lee's head-quarters; and that I wanted to find General Longstreet. The officer told us very demurely that he was going along in the right direction, and if we would accompany him he would show us the road. We thought that we now had the best of the bargain; and the citizens who had so tormented us smiled grimly as we rode off. After riding for some distance without anything being said, I asked our escort whether we were nearing the place to which we were going, and he replied in the affirmative. Passing through a thick skirt of woods, he suddenly wheeled to the right, and ordered us to follow him. We did so; and a few paces further on we saw the body of a man dangling from the bough of a tree; a halter having been used instead of a rope, to swing the poor devil up by. Asking what this meant, I was told that the dead man was a spy, and that all spies were treated in that way in this army. I was glad to receive the information, but did not see that it had any personal application until we reached a tent in front of which a stern looking man, in a General's uniform, was lolling on the ground. The officer dismounted, saluted, and said: "General, here are two men who have been arrested by some citizens of Stevensburg on suspicion of being spies." "Ah, indeed," said the General, rising with some interest. "What proofs have you of this?" "No particular proofs, General; but they refuse to show any papers, or to give any account of themselves." "Well!" said the General, "that's the best proof in the world. I have a short way of dealing with these rascals."

Then turning to a courier who was standing by, he said:
" Tell Captain ——— to detail a non-commissioned officer
and three men to report to me immediately." Turning to
us he kindly said : " Fine morning ! men. Any message or
any other little thing that you would like to send to your
friends in the North ?" Captain Taylor and I had been so
completely taken aback that, up to this time, we had said
nothing ; but the joke was becoming rather serious, and I
said frankly that Captain Taylor and I had refused to show
our papers because they had been asked for impertinently,
and without any authority ; but that we had in our pockets
our orders and our passports, and that I had letters of introduction to General Longstreet from General Randolph and
Colonel Gorgas. The order for the detail was counter-
manded as soon as our papers had been glanced at ; but
our friend, the General, told us that it was a suspicious circumstance, as we must admit, to find two officers of artillery
wandering about the country without any command, and on
foot. I suspect the nautical bearing of Captain Taylor,
which his uniform did not disguise, and my own fresh color
and English accent, had more to do with our trouble than
the fact that we were dismounted and alone. I really had
some little difficulty in making myself understood at Stevensburg. When I asked for water at the house, the man
hesitated until I had repeated the word two or three times ;
and then asked if I meant " wat-ter." We started off again,
and I parted from Captain Taylor, who went to General
Lee's head-quarters, while I plodded along to Brandy Station. I had seen Captain Taylor for the last time. He was
killed in action soon afterwards.

Almost broken down, I was trudging wearily along the
road when I heard some one bawling out my name. Look-

ing around I found that it was Lieutenant McGraw, of the Purcell Battery. In a minute or two I was in comfort and at ease in the midst of my old comrades. I had not seen Captain Willie Pegram since the fight at Mechanicsville, and we had a great deal of news to tell each other. The battery was parked in the woods, and, although we had no supper, I slept without waking. In the morning there was an artillery duel with the enemy at the Rappahannock River, in which we lost one or two men. Willie Pegram then lent me a poor old rip of a horse, with a hole in his side, punched there at Gaines' Mill by a piece of a shell; and I sallied forth once more to find General Longstreet. By this time I was about half starved, and I was very much disgusted by a soldier whom I met at the road-side with a huge pile of corn-dodgers, and who refused to sell me a piece of bread, although I offered him $5 for it. But I found General Longstreet at last, and was introduced by him to his Chief Ordnance Officer, Colonel Peyton L. Manning, who directed me to return to Brandy Station, where I should find the Ordnance train of the corps.

About night I found the train, and met with a cordial reception at the hands of Lieutenants Leech and Duxberry. A good supper of coffee, biscuit, and fried bacon was improvised, and I heartily enjoyed the quiet luxury of a pipe.

XIV.

A day or two after my arrival at my post, I succeeded in buying a very good riding horse, and hired a capable servant. I may as well say just here that I found Colonel Manning, my immediate superior, an exceedingly easy man to get along with. Unquestionably a gentleman in his tastes and habits, and brave as a lion, he knew comparatively little of his work as Ordnance officer, and was unable to write an ordinary official letter correctly. Spelling was indeed his weakest point. He was from Aberdeen, Miss., and died at his home there three or four years after the surrender. Lieutenant Leech was from Charlottesville, Va., and was very quiet and unassuming. Lieutenant Duxberry was good tempered, but exceedingly conceited, and casting about always to make himself friends at head-quarters. One of his peculiar conceits was that his name, Duxberry, was a corruption of Duc de Berri, from whom he supposed himself to be in some extraordinary way descended. I found out afterwards that, at the beginning of the war, he was an assistant in a drug store at Montgomery, Ala., and that he was born somewhere in Massachusetts.

Longstreet pressed through Thoroughfare Gap and reached Manassas just in time to save Jackson from being overwhelmed there. I knew but little of what was going on, and did not see much of the great battle itself. Here I made my first capture in the shape of a Gatling gun which had been abandoned by the enemy, and what was of more importance, I secured a commissary wagon containing a barrel of ground coffee.

The army now advanced to the Potomac, which we

crossed at Point of Rocks; the bands playing "Maryland, my Maryland!" There was no cause to complain any longer of a lack of provisions, and we were able to buy whatever we wanted with Confederate money at fair prices. After resting a day or two at Hagerstown, where we completed the equipment of our mess, we moved rapidly to South Mountain, where we had a brisk fight, and were driven back. This was on August 15th, I think. Late at night I rode back to the camp to get some supper, but had hardly told the cook to make the necessary preparations when an order came from General Longstreet to me to take charge of the Ordnance trains of the corps, and move them to Williamsport. The order was imperative, and I was directed to move as rapidly as possible.

At about ten o'clock at night I started. It was intensely dark and the roads were rough. Towards morning I entered the Hagerstown and Williamsport Turnpike, where I found a cavalry picket. The officer in charge asked me to move the column as quickly as I could, and to keep the trains well closed up. I asked him if the enemy were on the road, and he told me that it was entirely clear, and that he had pickets out in every direction. It was only a few miles now to Williamsport, and I could see the camp-fires of our troops across the river. I was hungry, sleepy and tired, and the prospect of camp and supper in an hour seemed the summit of bliss. I was forty or fifty yards ahead of the column, when a voice from the roadside called out "halt!" The gloss was not yet off my uniform, and I could not suppose that such a command, shotted with a big oath, was intended for me. In a moment it was repeated. I quickly rode to the side of the road in the direction of the voice, and found myself at the entrance of a narrow lane, and there adown it were horses and men in a line that stretched out far beyond my vision. To the trooper who was nearest to me I said indignantly: "How dare you halt an officer in this manner." The reply was to the point : "Surrender, and dismount! You are my prisoner!" Almost before the words were uttered I was surrounded, and found that I had ridden right into the midst of a body of Yankee cavalry, numbering about two thousand, who had escaped from Harper's Ferry that night to avoid the surrender which was to take place in the morning. I was placed under guard on the roadside, and as the trains came up they were halted, and the men who were with them were quietly captured. In a short time the column moved off in the direction of the Pennsylvania line. I was allowed to ride my own horse. By the side of each team a Federal soldier rode, and, by dint of cursing the negro drivers and beating the mules with their swords, the cavalrymen contrived to get the jaded animals along at a gallop. While we were halted, one of my Sergeants had knocked the linchpins out of the wheels of the leading wagons, in the hope that this would delay the march. The wheels came off and the wagons were upset, but a squad of men dismounted instantly, threw the wagons out of the road, and set fire to them, so that there was no halt of consequence. I had a cavalryman on each side of me, and tried vainly to get an opportunity to slip off into the woods.

9

XV.

Soon after daylight we reached the little village of Green-castle, Pennsylvania, where the citizens came out to look at the "Rebel" prisoners. They hurrahed for their own men and cursed at us. Even the women joined in the game. Several of them brought their children to the roadside and told them to shake their fists at the "d—d Rebels." Still there were some kind people in Greencastle. Three or four ladies came to us, and, without pretending to have any liking for Confederates, showed their charitable disposi-tion by giving us some bread and a cup of cold water. My horse was taken from me at Greencastle and ridden off by a dirty-looking cavalryman. Then the Confederates, num-bering a hundred or more, were packed into the cars, and sent by the railway to Chambersburg.

Duxberry had the good luck to be away from camp the night that we marched from Crampton's Gap, and was not taken. Leech had been asleep in one of the wagons, and did not wake up until we had all been gathered in.

Chambersburg is a pretty little town, and I had the satis-faction of seeing it a year later under pleasanter auspices. On arriving there the first time, the Confederates were put in the open yard of the jail which we pretty well filled. Our presence there suggested a new and interesting game to the small boys of Chambersburg. It was a plain calcula-tion that a stone which should fall within the area of the yard would be very apt to hit one of the prisoners. The boys, therefore, amused themselves by pitching stones over from the outside, enjoying in this way the luxury of scaring the "Rebels," and hurting them too, without any risk to themselves. It was sport to the boys, but it came near being death to some of our men. But here, as at Greencastle, there were some charitable souls. Mr. A. K. McClure, who is now the editor of the Philadelphia *Times*, came to the jail with a committee of citizens, and gave us an abundance of coffee and bread and meat. That night we lay on the rough stones in the jail yard, and in the morning we were put on the train for Harrisburg. We did not go into the town, but were taken at once to Camp Curtin, in the suburbs, where we were to remain until our final destination should be determined on.

By this time I had no baggage. It had been promised that my valise, which was in one of the wagons, should be given to me, but it was appropriated, I suppose, by one of our captors. At all events, I saw nothing of it, and could get no information about it.

At Camp Curtin we were tolerably comfortable. There were only two officers in our party besides myself, and as my uniform was comparatively bright and fresh I attracted more attention than my rank warranted. The United States officers at the camp were exceedingly attentive, and talked with me in the frankest manner about the position of affairs and the prospects of their army. They gave me a blanket which I needed sorely, and bestowed upon me what was equally desirable, a new tooth-brush. The evening after my arrival, the Commandant of the camp asked me whether I would not like to go into town, saying that one of the officers was anxious to take me in with him. I told him I had no other dress than my uniform, and if I had I would not wear it, and I did not suppose that any of the officers would care to go into Harrisburg with a Confederate officer in uniform. The Commandant said that this was what was proposed, although he did not think it very prudent. The Commandant gave me the necessary pass, and Captain ———— and I went into the town.

First we went into the principal hotel and took supper. The persons hanging about the hotel looked at me rather sulkily, but I was too hungry to pay much attention to them. After supper we walked out to the front of the hotel, where my companion slapped me on the shoulder, and said in a loud voice: " Here is a real live Rebel officer! The first man that says a word to him I will knock his d—d head off!" This was not a very pacific speech to make to a crowd of fanatical Pennsylvanians, who had just heard that the battle of Sharpsburg had begun. Nothing came of it at the moment, and my companion now insisted that we should visit the principal music hall. As we entered, the whole company of singers was on the stage shouting lustily: " The Union and McClellan forever! Three cheers for the Buck-tail Brigade," the audience joining in the chorus with patriotic energy. My companion marched me down the middle of the hall to the very front seat, and there was a murmur of astonishment and disapprobation. But my companion did not mind it, and I could not help it, so we remained there about half an hour and then passed out, with no other damage than being scowled at by the audience. By this time my companion was decidedly exhilarated; and the next time that he invited an attack, by saying that he would inflict condign punishment on any one who molested me, an indignant patriot knocked my hat off. I knocked down the man who did it, and half a dozen men pitched into me at once. There was a general scrimmage. Knives were drawn, a shot was fired, and I knew nothing more until I found myself in a large room surrounded by a group of

soldiers. In the row, it seemed, my companion had been
treated rather badly, and I had been choked and knocked
until I was insensible, and, indeed, was only saved from
death by a woman, who seized the arm of my foremost as-
sailant and prevented him from stabbing me to the heart.
Just as I had learned the particulars, the door opened and
an officer came in whom I recognized as the Commandant
of Camp Curtin. He said very quietly: "I thought you
would be very apt to bring up at the guard-house about
this time, so I came in to look after you." He then accompanied me back to camp. I did not wish to trouble the
Commandant to escort me to my quarters, but he told me
that his guards were quite young, rather stupid, and very
malicious, and quite apt to shoot at a stray prisoner without
giving him a chance to halt and explain. I objected no
further. The whole night's work was a very unpleasant
one for me, but I had no way of escaping from the difficulty
when I once reached the city. Captain ——— had been
drinking hard, which I had not suspected until it was too
late. If I had left him and gone off alone I should have
been in worse case than by remaining in his company.

The next morning the Harrisburg paper had a glowing
account of an attempt I had made to escape from camp,
and said that, when recaptured, I had nearly succeeded in
laying a mine to blow up the great bridge across the Sus-
quehannah. The newspapers, too, were very severe in their
condemnation of the Union officers who had been seen in
the city in company with a "Rebel officer in full uniform."

Early the next day we were ordered to be ready to take
the cars for Philadelphia, on the way to Fort Delaware. Just
before leaving camp, I was told that there were some ladies
at the gate who desired to see me. I went down and found

two handsomely dressed women in an open carriage. One of them asked me whether I did not recognize her. I told her that I did not, and she said: "You ought to do so, for I was passing by when you got into that difficulty in town, and was the means of saving your life." I thanked her very warmly, but told her that there were too many demands on my attention at the time of the fight to permit me to have seen her. The ladies bade me very heartily good bye, and I left my unknown friends.

It was not a long run to Philadelphia, and in the cars was a civilian who accosted me courteously, and asked me many questions about the Confederacy and the Southern people, the character of the army and the estimation in which the different Generals were held. All such questions I answered as well as I could without divulging anything that might be of injury to our side, and taking care to depict everything in the highest possible colors. It was night when the train reached the Quaker City, and I suppose that ten thousand persons were awaiting the arrival of the train. There were no lamps in the cars, and the persons in the crowd outside clambered up at the windows, even lighting matches and holding lanterns to our heads that they might see us the better, as though we were wild beasts in a cage. One man thrust his hand in through the sash, grasped my hand firmly and whispered: "Cheer up, it will all come out right." At last, it was my turn to leave the cars, and, as usual, my scarlet cap attracted more attention than was agreeable. Some said I was a drummer-boy, others declared I was a Colonel, while one big fellow shouted out that he knew that I was a spy who had deserted from the Union Army, and had been recaptured. There was instantly a shout: "Hang him to the lamp-post," and for a few minutes I was in worse plight at Philadelphia than I had been in at Stevensburg. The guard, however, succeeded in driving the crowd back, and I reached in safety the steamer which was to take us to Fort Delaware.

XVI.

Late at night we reached the Island upon which Fort Delaware is built. We were marched up to the gates, and were halted there until an officer had passed along the line and enquired whether any of the prisoners wished to take the oath of aliegiance to the United States government. There was no reply, and we were marched into the Barracks. These Barracks were common wooden sheds, affording accommodation for about ten thousand persons. The bunks were arranged in tiers of three, and into one of these I crawled. The next morning I was told that these Barracks were the quarters for the privates and non-commissioned officers, and that, by requesting it, I could be removed to the quarters for the officers, which were inside the Fort. Lieutenant Leech and I wrote to the Commandant, and were at once removed to the Fort, where we were installed in a large barrack-room, which then contained seventy or eighty officers. The highest in rank was a Major Holliday, belonging to one of the Virginia regiments.

During the time that I was in the Fort I slept next to Adjutant W. P. DuBose, of the Holcombe Legion, who had been taken prisoner at South Mountain. He was supposed to have been killed, but had really been but slightly wound ed. When he returned to South Carolina he found that his obituary had been published, and that his friends were in mourning for him. Afterwards he went into the ministry, and was appointed Chaplain of Kershaw's Brigade. He is now one of the Professors of the University of the South, at Sewanee.

As the number of officers increased with new arrivals, the

room became painfully crowded. Within the room we could do pretty much as we pleased, except that we were not allowed to gather together in a body, lest we might plan an escape, I suppose. Nor were we allowed to cross the threshold of the door, on pain of being shot. The guards were abusive, and would swear at us like dogs if we did anything they disapproved of. A word in reply was met by a blow with the butt end of a musket, or by an order that the offender be sent to the Black Hole. Still we were far better off than our comrades were in the Barracks outside. Our room was dry, warm and well lighted, while the Barracks were cold, damp and dark. Our room had conveniences for washing to a certain extent, and there was plenty of water of a poor quality. The washing of clothes went on all the time, which was not conducive to the comfort of those who used the washstand for personal ablutions. The inhabitants of the garments which were steeped in the washstand naturally took refuge in the water.

No exercise of any kind was permitted to us, and we only left the room to march down into the mess-hall. For breakfast we had a cup of poor coffee without milk or sugar, and two small pieces of bad bread. For dinner we had a cup of greasy water misnamed soup, a piece of beef two inches square and a half inch thick, and two slices of bread. At supper the fare was the same as at breakfast. This was exceedingly light diet. Some of the officers behaved disagreeably; and eight or ten of us, principally Virginians, associated ourselves together for mutual protection, and formed a mess of our own. We contrived to make some additions to our diet by purchases at the Sutler's store. When we had no money the Sutler would take watches or other valuables in pledge, and let us have the provisions.

10

A number of the citizens of Baltimore, including Mr. Carpenter, had been arrested for disloyalty, and they were found at this time in the Fort. They were not watched as closely as we were, and sometimes in going down to dinner we had an opportunity to exchange a word with them. They were jolly fellows, and exceedingly liberal. Mr. Carpenter was editor of the Maryland *News Sheet,* and was released about the time of our arrival. 'Being appointed the chairman of the Baltimore Society for the relief of prisoners, he returned to the Fort to see what our wants were. At one shipment over two thousand pair of excellent shoes were sent to the Fort for the prisoners. Indeed, each one of the three thousand Confederates in the Fort received a blanket, a pair of shoes, warm trousers, a jacket, and a felt hat; or such of these things as he required. Nor were the officers in our room forgotten. Clothing of every kind was sent to us. It was proposed at first that the senior officer present should take charge of the supplies, and distribute the clothing according to the necessities of the individuals. This did not suit some of our comrades. When the packages were brought in and opened there was a general rush, and those who pulled hardest and pushed most got the larger part of the spoils. I saw men wear two pair of new trousers under an old pair, and then complain to Mr. Carpenter that they wanted a new pair. And so it was with jackets and with under-clothing. Blankets were in great demand. One man who was crying lustily for a blanket was found to have four new blankets hidden under his bunk.

I had only been in the Fort a day or two when the guard called my name, and handed me a newspaper. This was a most unusual occurrence, as newspapers were not allowed to be given to us, unless they contained some startling re-

port of Union victories. The newspaper was the Philadelphia *Inquirer*, a rabid Union sheet, and I was curious to
see what it contained that concerned me. There I saw, in
big type, the announcement of "The Arrival of the Rebel
Prisoners!" "Conversation with a Rebel Officer of Longstreet's Staff!" "Condition of the South!" "What is
thought of the Rebel Generals!" &c., &c. The writer said
that, in the cars, he had had the pleasure of a conversation
with Lieutenant Dawson, of General Longstreet's Staff, who
was in England when the war began, but immediately returned to his home in Sussex County, Va., and entered the
Confederate service! After complimenting me upon my
intelligence and courtesy, he gave a very fair report of what
I said. The mystery was explained. My inquisitive friend
on the cars was a newspaper reporter. I was annoyed by
the publicity given to what I had said, for I feared that my
friends at the South would misunderstand it; but it proved
after all to be a fortunate occurrence for me. Two days
after the appearance of the article in the Philadelphia *Inquirer*, the guard came and began to talk to me in a surpris-
ingly civil way. Suddenly he turned his back to me and
slipped a letter into my hand, telling me not to let any one
see it. I hurried off to the only private place we had, and
read my letter. It was from a Mr. Neal, of Walnut Street,
Philadelphia. He said that he had seen my name in the
Inquirer, and that, being a Virginian and a prisoner, I had
claims upon him; and that anything that I wanted, either
in money or clothes, he would be only too happy to send
me. I replied, thanking him for his kindness, and asking
that he would send me some under-clothing, of which I
stood in great need. Mr. Neal at once came down to the
Fort, and brought me a valise well furnished with handker-

chiefs, socks, shirts, collars, and other things that I required. He also insisted that I should take a small sum of money, which I was fortunately able to return to him when I was set at liberty. Much to my regret, I have not been able to learn anything about Mr. Neal since the war ended.

I had hardly settled down to the quiet enjoyment of my valise and its contents, when a big basket was brought to me, with a note from a Miss Spotswood, who said she saw by the papers that I was from Sussex, Virginia, where she had spent many happy years, and begged that in memory of this I would accept the accompanying basket. I did. In the basket were jelly, preserves, sugar, tea, coffee, pickles, pepper and salt, a comb and brush, a tooth-brush, note paper, envelopes and postage stamps. My comfort was now complete. Who but a woman would have thought of sending so many little necessaries which I could not otherwise have obtained!

XVII.

The time dragged heavily, although we amused ourselves by singing Southern songs and playing games, some very pretty chess-men and chequers having been made by the prisoners. There were cards in abundance, and there was a faro-bank; but these games were not patronized by our mess. Once on a Sunday we were allowed to go to Church service on the ramparts, but this privilege was not granted again.

The confinement had a serious effect upon me, and I became really unwell; but new courage was given to all of us by the rumor that there would soon be a general exchange of prisoners, and that we should be released on parole. The rumor gained ground; but day after day passed and no confirmation came. When we had almost given up hope, an Orderly announced to us that Major Burton, the Commandant, had sent a message to us, which he would deliver if we would receive it quietly. In a moment all was still: "Major Burton says that orders have been received from Washington to send you all on to Virginia to be exchanged, as soon as boats can be secured." We could not restrain the cheers that rose to our lips.

A day or two afterwards, when we began to think that we had been deceived, the printed forms of parole were brought in for signature. This part of the performance having been completed, Major Holliday, the senior officer, was called for, and went out. Shortly afterwards one of the Captains was taken away; then another Captain was sent for. When five or six had gone out and none had returned, so that all the tracks went one way, we began to

wonder what it meant. My name was next called. I went
out, and was conducted to Major Burton's office, where was
an officer in full uniform. Major Burton said that Colonel
———, of the United States Army, wished to speak with
me. The Colonel asked me whether I was on General
Longstreet's staff. I told him I was. He then asked me
how many divisions there were on General Longstreet's
command. I did not answer him. He repeated the question, and asked how many men Longstreet had. My reply
was: "You have no right to ask such questions; and you
cannot suppose that I shall so far forget my duty as an
officer, and my honor as a gentleman, as to tell you anything
whatever concerning the command to which I belong."
Again being asked the question with the same result, I
was given up as a bad job, and told that I could return to
my quarters. Hurrying back to the room, taking on the
way a bag of cakes that some sweet Maryland girls offered
me, I reached the room and found the men there in great
excitement, as no one of those who had been called out had
come back. I described what was going on, and bade them
be on their guard. By this time it had been ascertained
that I had returned to our quarters instead of retiring to
the room where were placed the other officers who had been
catechized. So I was hurried out again, and unceremoniously put in the pen. The object was to keep the officers
in our quarters in ignorance of what was expected to be ex-
tracted from them. But the hint I had had time to give
was sufficient. Thenceforward the haughty Colonel received free answers to his questions; but I am not disposed to
think that the information was very valuable. He asked
particularly the number of Maryland troops in our service,
and one officer told him that we now had fifty thousand

Maryland Infantry, ten thousand Cavalry, and five battalions of Artillery. The interrogator was astonished. He said he had thought that there were only one or two thousand Maryland troops in our service, which was near the truth. The officer told him that of late all the Marylanders in the different Brigades had been consolidated into a Maryland Corps, which had the strength stated. A special note was taken of this information. Another officer belonged to a Brigade which had about four hundred muskets, and was asked the strength of it. He asked whether his interrogator wanted to know its present strength or the usual strength. The Colonel said he wanted to know both. The officer told him that the usual strength was about twenty-two hundred men, but he reckoned it had not more than eighteen hundred men now.

At last the long expected steamers came, and we went aboard. Our confinement was at an end, and only the sea trip and the run up the James River lay before us. The Sutler tried hard to play a Yankee trick. I have mentioned that we pawned watches and chains with him in order to buy provisions. Prior to the time for leaving the Fort most of us had obtained the money to redeem them. Major Burton indeed offered to furnish us any small sum that we needed, which we might remit to him when we reached home. But the Sutler, as soon as he learned that we were going away, went up to Philadelphia, and did not return. It was evident that he intended to remain absent until we were out of reach ; but the boats were later in arriving than he expected, and he was obliged to come back to his post. Our pledges were redeemed, and the Sutler received a severe rebuke from Major Burton. No one could have been more considerate, consistently with his duty, than Major Burton

was. This is the same noble officer who had President
Davis in charge, after he was taken from the custody of the
brutal officer who caused him to be so tortured at Fortress
14 Monroe, as described in Dr. Craven's well known book.
Mrs. Burton was, I think, a Mexican lady, and sympathized
very deeply with the Southerners. One day while we were
on our way to the mess-hall, she waved her handkerchief to
us, but I suppose that the good Major was constrained to
prevent so unwise demonstrations afterwards. We did not
see her again.

The fresh sea breeze was very refreshing, and we sat up
nearly all night talking of home. Hunger, however, soon
asserted itself, and we had much difficulty in getting a small
piece of cold pork and some hard-tack. The next evening
we reached Fortress Monroe, where we expected that our
baggage would be searched or confiscated; but by some
good fortune it was allowed to pass, and we reached Varina,
ten miles below Richmond, without any trouble, although
nearly famished.

Our commissioner of exchange was expected to meet us,
but he was at church in Richmond with some fair lady, or
too happily engaged otherwise to hurry down to attend to
the wants of a few hundred prisoners who were half starved
and pining to be ashore again. So we remained many hours
within ten paces of the shore, before the necessary forms
were complied with and we were allowed to land. There
was some talk of sending us to Camp Lee to remain there
until we should be exchanged; but I was taken by a friend
in his carriage to Richmond, where we arrived at night. I
was surprised that my joy at my deliverance was not so
visible on my face that it would be noticed on the streets,
and I half expected that even strangers would congratulate

me.   It was the 6th of October when I reached Richmond.
I had been a prisoner of war only three weeks, but it seemed
to me an eternity, and I can hardly realize now that the time,
counted by days and weeks, was really so short.   And yet,
it must have been so.

11

XVIII.

The morning after my arrival at Richmond, I went down to the head-quarters of General G. W. Smith, who was then in command of the Department of Richmond, and asked his Adjutant-General for leave of absence until I should be exchanged. The Adjutant-General, who was no less a person than Major Samuel W. Melton, of South Carolina, refused point blank to allow me to leave the city. The officers and men who had been paroled could not, of course, rejoin their commands until they should have been exchanged, and there seemed to be no object in keeping them in Richmond. It was feared, however, that if they were allowed to go home, some of them might not return promptly; and for this reason no leaves were to be granted. As usual in such cases, the many were to suffer for the possible faults of the few. In my own case there was certainly no reason to refuse a leave of absence, as if I had desired to leave the service I could have done so at any time by resigning. The Conscript law of course did not affect me, and it seemed rather absurd to suppose that one who was in the Confederate service by his own choice would keep away from the field of duty which he had deliberately selected. I went to my friend, Colonel Gorgas, the Chief of Ordnance, made my official report of the capture of the trains at Williamsport, and through him obtained from the Secretary of War permission to go down to Sussex, and remain there until the completion of the exchange of the paroled prisoners.

After remaining at Petersburg a few days, I went on to Sussex, and found my friends there in great distress. Mrs. Raines had died the day before my arrival, and the loss to her husband and family seemed irreparable. To me, also, it was a heavy blow, for Mrs. Raines had been to me from the beginning a good and true friend. I stayed awhile with Major Belsches, about two miles away, and then went over to Oakland, where I had the complete rest and quiet I so much needed. The change from the dreary confinement and brutal treatment at Fort Delaware to the ease and abundance at Oakland was sufficient to make any one happy.

The days passed swiftly by, and it was not until the latter part of November that I was exchanged and free to return to the army. A fresh horse was now necessary, and I bought in Petersburg, for $400, a good-looking black charger, which turned out to be an utterly good-for-nothing animal. From Petersburg, I rode, by way of Richmond, to Fredericksburg, where General Longstreet now was. I reported for duty on December the 6th, and set to work at once to familiarize myself with the condition of my department. Lieutenant Leech did not return to us, but was assigned to duty with General Pickett as Chief of Ordnance of the division. Lieutenant Duxberry I found at head-quarters in much the same condition as when I left him at South Mountain. Very soon, the whole responsibility in the Ordnance Department of Longstreet's Corps devolved upon me. Colonel Manning had no taste for anything but marching and fighting, and Lieutenant Duxberry was too fond of pleasure and show to be of much practical use.

I was under canvas at this time a few hundred yards from Guinea Station. The weather was bitterly cold, but my tent was small, and with the aid of a large stove I managed to keep reasonably warm. There was, as yet, no particular deficiency in the Commissary Department, but there was not much variety in the food. Bacon was the great staple, with occasional rations of beef, so tough that it deserved to be described, as it once was, as "the sinews of war." The fat of the bacon was used in place of lard, in making bread and biscuits, so that when the bacon itself was served it was particularly dry. There was so great a craving for a change in the food that I ate often with relish a sauce composed of bacon fat and brown sugar, which in these days is sickening to think of. One of my men captured somewhere a keg of lard which proved to be a great acquisition. I think I may safely say that it was not paid for.

XIX.

The battle of Fredericksburg was at hand. I need not describe it, except to say that from Howison's Hill, afterwards known as Lee's Hill, where Generals Lee and Longstreet and their staffs remained for a considerable part of the day, there was a magnificent view of as grand a spectacle as one could desire to see in war. I was there soon after daybreak, and as the mist of the morning cleared away we could easily make out the enemy's movements. Large bodies of troops had already crossed the Rappahannock, and the fields near it were blue with Yankees. On the opposite shore were the long trains of wagons and ambulances, together with the reserve artillery. A 30-pound Parrot gun which we had was ordered to open on the enemy, and very soon the artillery fire became brisk. Fredericksburg, which had been so calm and peaceful in the early light, was set on fire by the enemy's shells. The enemy now made a fierce attack on our right, which was repulsed with comparative ease. It was thrilling to watch the long line advance, note the gaps in the array, as the wounded fell or else staggered to the rear, and see the gallant remnant melt away like snow before our withering fire. At Marye's Hill, which was the key to our position, the most desperate fighting was done. Again and again the enemy charged, only to be driven back with terrible slaughter. There it was that Meagher's Brigade made its historic charge. The field in front of the hill, beyond the road, was well called the slaughter-pen. The enemy lay there in their ranks, as they had fallen, and the fence was riddled like a sieve by the rifle bullets. I had a very narrow escape. Standing in a group with three other officers watching the action, a shell exploded near us and bruised or wounded everyone of my companions. I was not touched.

Late at night I returned to camp, and crept into a wagon to take a quiet sleep, placing my coat, cap and trousers under my head, in the front part of the wagon. In the morning my coat was missing, and the natural conclusion was that it had been stolen. Such things did happen. Looking about rather disconsolately, and wondering how I was to replace the missing garment, I saw some buttons and shreds of gold lace lying on the ground. The thieves were discovered. It was the wretched mules, who had unceremoniously dragged my clothes out of the wagon and chewed up my uniform coat, in place of the long forage, the hay or fodder, which they craved. The mules, at this time, were fed on corn almost exclusively; and their desire for rough food, as it was called, led them frequently to gnaw the poles of the wagons. These poles on this account were protected in many cases by strips of iron, which rendered them impervious to even the teeth of a mule. I was in a sad dilemma, of course, and was laughed at for my pains. Fortunately, I succeeded in buying a coat, which answered my purposes until I reached Petersburg, in the spring.

The army was now into winter quarters, the men making themselves as comfortable as they could. Snow-balling was a favorite amusement, and was carried on in grand style, brigade challenging brigade to a sham fight. These contests were very exciting, and were the source of great amusement to the men. Practical jokes, too, were frequently played upon the officers. Mrs. Longstreet was staying at a house a mile or two from our head-quarters, and General

Longstreet rode over there every evening, returning to camp in the morning. On his way he passed through the camp of the Texas Brigade of Hood's Division, and was frequently saluted with a shower of snow-balls. For sometime he took it with his usual imperturbability, but he grew tired of the one-sided play at last, and the next time that he was riding by the Texans, and found them drawn up on the side of the road, snow-balls in hand, he reined up his horse, and said to them very quietly: "Throw your snow-balls men, if you want to, as much as you please; but, if one of them touches me, not a man in this brigade shall have a furlough this winter. Remember that!" There was no more snow-balling for General Longstreet's benefit.

The officers at our head-quarters had a less innocent amusement than pitching snow-balls. The great American game of poker was played nearly every night. One of the most successful of the gamesters was Major Walton, who was a kinsman of General Longstreet, through whose influence he had received an appointment in the Commissary Depart- ment. He really did general staff duty. At one sitting Walton won $2,000 or more from Dr. Maury, who was one of the Surgeons of the corps; and he caused much un- favorable comment by sending to Dr. Maury for his win- nings before that gentleman was out of bed in the morning. There was hard drinking as well as high playing; and it was reported that at the close of one debauch General Longstreet had played horse with one of the stronger officers of his staff, who on all-fours carried Longstreet around and around the tent until the pair of them rolled over on the ground together.

The head-quarters of General Lee were in the woods, and far from luxurious. He was advised by his physicians to stay in one of the houses near by, as many of his officers were doing, but he declined to fare any better than his men did. There was no pomp or circumstance about his head-quarters, and no sign of the rank of the occupant, other than the Confederate flag displayed in front of the tent of Colonel Taylor, the Adjutant-General.

It may not be out of place to mention the scale of prices that prevailed in the Confederacy towards the close of the year 1862, as I gave them in a letter to my mother: Shoes $30 a pair; common calico shirts $10 each; socks $1 a pair; butter $2 a pound; turkeys $15 each; matches 50 to 75 cents a box; ink 25 cents a bottle; blacking $1 a cake; writing paper $2 a quire.

XX.

Early in 1863 Longstreet was placed in command of the Department of Virginia and North Carolina, with headquarters at Petersburg, and with Hood's and Pickett's Divisions he moved to that place. An effort to capture Suffolk, on the Norfolk and Petersburg Railroad, was contemplated, and most of our command moved in that direction. I remained at Petersburg during the operations, which were unsuccessful.

It was, of course, very pleasant for me in the Cockade City, and my pay had accumulated sufficiently to permit me to provide myself with new uniforms, in the latest style and at extravagant prices.

There was considerable excitement in the city, in consequence of an order that the pleasure horses of the citizens should be impressed for the use of the artillery. To this there was a very decided objection, and every manner of device was resorted to save the pet animals. Some good people attempted to run off their horses into the country, but pickets had been stationed along the roads and the fugitives were easily captured. When the impressing officers went around to examine the horses in town, they found horses in the cellars and even in the dining-rooms. A carriage containing three ladies and drawn by a pair of fine bay horses was going down Sycamore Street when a guard ordered the driver to halt, and told the ladies that it was his unpleasant duty to impress the team. The ladies, who were young and pretty, declared that the horses should not be taken. They tried both entreaty and expostulation, but the guard was inexorable. The ladies then declared that.

12

if the horses were taken they must be taken too, and thought
they had gained the victory. The guard did go away,
but he quietly unhitched the traces, and took the horses
with him, leaving the ladies in their carriage in all their
glory. In some cases the impressment was useless, as delicate horses were taken which were of no use for service in
the field.

The battle of Chancellorsville had been fought during our
stay around Petersburg, and the command was then hurried
back to the neighborhood of Fredericksburg. It was in
May, 1863, I think, that I returned there. The Gettysburg
campaign began, but before this I saw the review of the
whole cavalry of the army at Brandy Station. The enemy
came in upon us shortly afterwards, and, in the very beginning of the cavalry fighting, Colonel Sol. Williams, of the
1st North Carolina, was killed. He had been married to
Miss Maggie Pegram, Captain Robert B. Pegram's eldest
daughter, only about two weeks before. The Adjutant of
his regiment was John Pegram, Captain Pegram's eldest
son, who was killed at Petersburg in 1864.

The march from Culpepper Court House through Chester
Gap, in the Blue Ridge, was very delightful to me, as the
weather was fine and the scenery was beautiful. I was
particularly struck with the scenery at Front Royal and
Shenandoah. The Valley of Virginia then showed few signs
of war.

This time we crossed the Potomac at Williamsport. It
was a dreary day! The rain was falling in torrents.
General Lee, General Longstreet and General Pickett were
riding together, followed by their staffs. When we reached
the Maryland shore we found several patriotic ladies with
small feet and big umbrellas waiting to receive the Confed-

erates who were coming a second time to deliver down-trodden Maryland. As General Lee rode out of the water, one of the ladies, with a face like a door-knocker, stepped forward and said: "This is General Lee, I presume?" General Lee gave an affirmative reply, and the lady continued: "General Lee, allow me to bid you welcome to Maryland, and allow me to present to you these ladies who were determined to give you this reception—Miss Brown, General Lee; Miss Jones, General Lee; Miss Smith, General Lee." General Lee thanked them courteously for their attention, and introduced General Longstreet and General Pickett to Miss Brown, Miss Jones and Miss Smith. This was not the end of the affair, however, as one of the ladies had an enormous wreath which she was anxious to place on the neck of General Lee's charger. The horse objected to it seriously, and the wreath was turned over to one of the couriers. The next morning we went into Hagerstown, where more ladies were in waiting. There were more presentations to General Lee and more introductions for Generals Longstreet and Pickett. One fair lady asked General Lee for a lock of his hair. General Lee said that he really had none to spare, and he was quite sure, besides, that they would prefer such a souvenir from one of his younger officers, and that he was confident that General Pickett would be pleased to give them one of his curls. General Pickett did not enjoy the joke, for he was known everywhere by his corkscrew ringlets, which were not particularly becoming when the rain made them lank in such weather as we then had. The ladies did not press the request. When we resumed our march more ladies came to be presented, but this time there were no petitions for a lock of Pickett's hair.

It was some satisfaction for me to pass once more through Greencastle, where I had been bedeviled by both men and women when taken there by the cavalry who captured me the year before. Thence we went to Chambersburg, and I was amazed to find that hundreds of sturdy well-dressed citizens were still in the town. In Virginia there was hardly a white man to be found who was not in the Confederate service, excepting the sick and those who were too old or too infirm for any sort of military duty; and it gave us a realizing sense of the strength of the enemy to see that they could have so large armies in the field and leave so many lusty men in peace at home.

The army behaved superbly in Pennsylvania. The orders against straggling and looting were strict, and they were cheerfully obeyed. It was on the march in Pennsylvania that I saw General Lee, one morning, dismount from his horse and replace the rails of the fence of a wheat field which had been thrown down by some of our men. It was the best rebuke that he could have given to the offenders.

At Chambersburg I paid a visit to the jail in which I had been confined, and found a number of Yankee soldiers in the yard. Had I been so minded, I might have played upon them the malicious trick of which the Chambersburg boys made us the objects when we were there. Riding through the town, I recognized one of the citizens who had been peculiarly kind to me when I was a prisoner, and who had given me then an excellent dinner. I thought I would catechise him a little, and called out in a loud voice: " Halt, there!" He seemed rather nervous, and asked what I would have. " Do you live here?" I asked. He said that he did. " Did you live here last year?" He replied in the affirmative. "Were you here in September last, when a number of Confederate prisoners were brought in?" He said, "Yes, I was, but I did nothing against them." Looking sternly at him I said, "Do you remember me?" He said that he did not. "Well, sir," I continued, "I was one of those prisoners." By this time he was badly frightened, and I hastened to relieve him by saying that my only object was to thank him for his kindness to me, and ascertain if there was anything I could do for him in return. He thanked me, but said that the town was so quiet that he needed no protection.

Late in the evening I rode out of the town, and it was dark before I came back. I was riding quite rapidly, and my horse, striking his foot against one of the stepping stones in the middle of the street, fell and threw me about ten feet over his head. As I went down I heard a woman exclaim: "Thank God, one of those wicked Rebels has broken his neck." I was not hurt, and my horse was not much injured, so I remounted and, riding to the sidewalk, informed my unseen foe that the pleasure she anticipated was, at least, postponed.

The people generally were evidently greatly surprised at the devotion of our men to General Lee, and made some rough remarks about it. One old lady called out to an officer of ours as he strode by: "You are marching mighty proudly now, but you will come back faster than you went." "Why so, old lady?" he asked. "Because you put your trust in General Lee and not in the Lord Almighty," she replied.

I should mention here that the horse which I was riding was a fine black gelding, which I had bought on our way to the Valley of Virginia. A more thoroughly trustworthy animal I could not have had, and he stood fire splendidly.

I had two other horses at this time, but always rode in action the black gelding I have just spoken of. I had intended to have given him some fancy name, but my boy Aleck dubbed him " Pete " the day I bought him, and by that name he went.

XXI.

On the march from Chambersburg we learned that General Meade had been placed in command of the Union Army, and we pushed on towards Gettysburg, where A. P. Hill's Corps had been heavily engaged. This day I was prostrated by sickness, and rode in an ambulance until nearly night, when I managed to get on my horse and go down to the battle-field. Longstreet himself has described admirably the fighting the next day; and, careless as he generally was of himself under fire, he nowhere else exposed himself more recklessly. One charge he led in person, and some prisoners whom we captured, when they learned who it was that had ridden in front of our advancing line, said they might expect to get whipped when a Corps commander exposed himself in that way to show his men how to fight.

The following day, July 3, the ever-memorable battle of Gettysburg was fought. Every arrangement was made to shell the enemy's position, on Cemetery Hill, and follow this up by an attack in force. The whole of the long range guns in the army were placed in battery along the low range of hills which we occupied, and at three o'clock the cannonading began. The enemy made prompt reply. Three or four hundred pieces of artillery were being fired as rapidly as the cannoneers could load them. Being in the centre of the front line, I had an excellent view of the fight. It was a hellish scene. The air was dotted with clouds of smoke where shells had burst, and the fragments of shell and the solid shot were screaming and shrieking in every direction. Through it all, General Longstreet was as unmoved as a statue, watching placidly the enemy's lines. In the meanwhile Pickett's Division had been formed in readiness for the charge. Three of his brigades were present; those of Kemper, Armistead and Garnett, composed exclusively of Virginians. Prayers were offered up in front of Armistead's brigade and Garnett's brigade, before the advance began. Garnett remarked to Armistead: "This is a desperate thing to attempt." Brave old Armistead replied: "It is; but the issue is with the Almighty, and we must leave it in his hands." Just then a hare which had been lying in the bushes, sprang up and leaped rapidly to the rear. A gaunt Virginian, with an earnestness that struck a sympathetic chord in many a breast, yelled out: "Run old heah; if I were an old heah I would run too." The artillery firing ceased, and the order to advance was given. Pickett was in the centre, with Wilcox's Division on the right, and Pender's, commanded by Pettigrew, on the left. The thin grey line of Virginians moved as steadily as on parade, the battle flags catching a deeper red from the sun. Well in front of their brigades were Kemper, and Garnett, and Armistead. The last named was bare-headed, his grey locks floating in the breeze. Waving his sabre and hat in hand, he cheered on his men. They did what men could do; but more had been expected of them than mortal men could accomplish. Armistead was mortally wounded inside the enemy's works. Garnett was killed instantly. Kemper was severely wounded, and supposed to be dying. My recollection is that only one field officer in Pickett's Division escaped unhurt.

The attack had been made and had failed. There was a terrible gap in our line, and the enemy threatened to advance. In the meanwhile the staff officers were busily engaged in rallying the men, who had made their way back

from the front.   I suppose that I was the first man to whom
Pickett spoke when he reached the line.   With tears in his
eyes, he said to me: "Why did you not halt my men here?
Great God, where, oh! where is my division?"   I told him
that he saw around him what there was left of it.   General
Lee, of course, took all the blame on himself.   As was well
said by a writer at this time: "General Lee was grand on
the smoke-crowned hills of Petersburg, on the sanguinary
field of Chancellorsville, and on the tragic plains of Manassas; but when at Gettysburg he told his men, 'It is my
fault', he rose above his race, and communed with the
angels of heaven."   That sad night not more than three
hundred men remained to us of what had been one of the
finest divisions in the service.   The remnants of the companies were commanded by corporals and sergeants; regiments by lieutenants; and a brigade by a Major.   Never
had Virginia suffered a heavier blow.   The division was
composed of the flower of her children, and there was weep-
ing and desolation in every part of the Old Dominion.

It was in every way an ugly time.   There was always
considerable difficulty in obtaining a sufficient supply of
artillery ammunition.   The first trouble was in making it,
and the second was in finding transportation for it.   At no
time did we have so large a reserve as was necessary.   What
was true of the artillery was true in a less degree of the
infantry.   There was even some delay on our march into
Pennsylvania in consequence of the detention of a train of
ordnance wagons, which did not arrive when expected.   A
brigade of infantry with a battery of artillery, was sent as
an escort; for had that train been captured it would have
been risking too much to advance farther.   The terrible
cannonade on the third day at Gettysburg exhausted the

13

whole of the artillery ammunition in reserve. My recollection is, that there was no long range ammunition left except what was in the caisons and limber chests. Under such circumstances, and having lost so heavily in the attack on Cemetery Hill, General Lee determined to retreat to Virginia; but we lay one day at least on the field awaiting the attack which Meade did not venture to make. The Union forces had suffered severely; but they could stand the loss of men better than we could; and they had a right to claim Gettysburg as a decisive victory, for we had failed utterly in what we had undertaken.

The march back to the Potomac was dreary and miserable indeed. The rain fell in torrents. The clothing of the men was worn and tattered, and too many of them were without shoes. It was a heart-breaking business, and gloom settled down upon the army. The enemy's cavalry made an attempt to cut us off at Williamsport, where the river was too high for fording, and they would have succeeded but for the gallantry of the wagoners and "Company Q" (the stragglers, and the disabled men with the trains), who had a free fight with them, and drove them back. We crossed the river on a pontoon bridge, leaving the cavalry in the entrenchments at Williamsport, and plodded our way back towards Winchester. Just about this time we received the news of the fall of Vicksburg. It needed only this to intensify the feeling that the star of the Confederacy was setting.

Passing from grave to gay, I may mention here that a sad trick was played on me by Captain Innes Randolph, an Engineer officer at our head-quarters. While we were at Bunker Hill, on the way to Winchester, he invited me to dine with him, saying that his mess had a very fine 'possum, which would be a novelty to me if I had not tasted that

succulent dish.   It was finely served, and merited the enco-
miums that Randolph lavished upon it.   He was careful,
besides, to tell me that I should find, as I did, that it tasted
very much like roast sucking pig.   Two or three years afterwards Randolph told me that this famous dish was not
possum after all, but a sucking pig which he had bagged in the
neighborhood, and which he had dubbed 'possum in order
to spare me the pain of banqueting on a dish that I knew
to be —— I was going to say "stolen," but we called it
"captured" in the army.

Resuming our march, we passed through Millwood and
Chester Gap, where we had a slight skirmish with the enemy.   One of our brigades charged across a field which was
thick with blackberry bushes.   The fruit was ripe, and as
the men moved forward firing they would pick the black-
berries and hastily eat them.   No troops ever showed more
indifference to danger, or took fighting more as a matter of
course, than the veterans of the Army of Northern Virginia.

We went into camp at Culpepper Court House, and remained there a considerable time.

XXII.

The army rapidly recovered its tone, and we heard that one corps of the three was to be sent to Tennessee. The choice fell upon Longstreet, who took with him Hood's and McLaws' Divisions of Infantry and Alexander's Battalion of Artillery. Pickett's Division was left in Virginia to recruit. There was much for me to do preparing for the change of base, and I was permitted to remain a day or two in Richmond on the way to the West. I stayed in Richmond at the house of Mr. John H. Tyler, the father of Henry Tyler, who was one of the Ordnance Sergeants with us, and a most excellent fellow. From the first time that I went to Richmond after I made his acquaintance, Mr. and Mrs. Tyler made their house like a home to me; and until the end of the war, and long afterward, a chair was kept as regularly for me at their table as though I had been one of their sons. Their generous and unaffected kindness to me, year after year, was more than I could ever hope to repay. God bless them.

I was a day or two later than the corps in leaving Richmond; but the cars were crowded with our soldiers, and when we reached South Carolina we received attentions which had long ceased to be common in Virginia, where the passage of large bodies of troops was an every day occurrence. At Sumter, South Carolina, a number of ladies were waiting for us on the platform, armed with bouquets of flowers and with well filled baskets of cake, fruit and more substantial fare. There was an abundance, too, of lemonade for the dusty soldiers. But the good things were for the soldiers only. Some ladies in the car were evidently faint with long fasting, and a civilian who was with them asked a very pretty girl, who had a large dish of cake and sandwiches, to give him a piece of the cake for a lady in the car who really needed it.   With the mercilessness which one woman usually shows to another, the fair young patriot told him jauntily that everything there was for the soldiers, and that ladies and civilians must look out for themselves. Our men were rather unaccustomed to so much kindness, in these days, but they enjoyed it thoroughly.   At Augusta, and at Atlanta, also, we were most hospitably received.

I overtook the command and General Longstreet shortly after their arrival at Chickamauga Station, and we had the satisfaction of knowing that it was "the Virginia troops," as they were called, to whom was mainly due the glory of the victory we won at Chickamauga.   Our loss was severe, and Colonel Manning, my immediate superior, was slightly wounded and placed *hors de combat*.   This left me in name, as in fact, in charge of the Ordnance Department of the corps.

I wish that I could remember precisely what took place the next day, when I went with Major Walton to find General McLaws, in the neighborhood of Chattanooga.   We were exceedingly anxious that he should drive right on after the enemy, but he made the objection at once that the movement might not be successful, and would be sure to be attended with heavy loss.   He said, however, that he would make the advance if we gave him an imperative order in General Longstreet's name to do so.   This order we declined to give, to my present regret, and General McLaws contented himself with asking General Longstreet to send him some more ambulances.   When we reached General Longstreet late that night, and told him what General

McLaws had said, his only remark was a wish that the ambulances were in a hotter place than Chattanooga. Longstreet did not love McLaws, and preferred charges against him afterwards for neglect of duty in the attack on Fort Sanders, at Knoxville.

The whole army came up, and the investment of Chattanooga began. Our head-quarters were in the low ground, which was always under water in winter, but we managed tolerably well as long as fine weather lasted. Soon the rain began to fall steadily, and it was a difficult matter so to arrange the ditches around our tents as to save ourselves from being washed away at night.

Frank Vizetelly, the artist and correspondent of the *Illustrated London Times*, joined us here; and with him was Captain Ross, of the Austrian service. Ross was of Scotch descent, but was born in Austria, and belonged to one of the crack light cavalry regiments. There was a good deal of merry-making, and it was no uncommon thing to see a half dozen officers, late at night, dancing the " The Perfect Cure," which was one of the favorite songs of the day in the London music halls, and was introduced to our notice by Vizetelly.

There were sharp discussions occasionally as to what should take place when the war should be over and the independence of the Confederate States was assured. Major Walton I had always disliked heartily, and in one of our conversations he said that, when the Confederate States enjoyed their own government, they did not intend to have any "d—d foreigners" in the country. I asked him what he expected to become of men like myself, who had given up their own country in order to render aid to the Confederacy. He made a flippant reply, which I answered rather warmly, and he struck at me. I warded off the blow, and slapped his face. The next morning I sent him a challenge by Captain Ross. Walton, however, did not want a fight at this time, and offered to make an ample apology in writing. A day or two passed, and as no apology came I sent Ross to him again. Walton now took the position that he had been hasty in his action, and that if he had not promised to do it he would not make an apology at all. Ross told him very quietly, in his quaint way, that he must please consider everything blotted out that had taken place since he had borne the challenge, and that we would begin it again at that point and settle the affair in any way that Walton preferred. This brought Walton to terms, and he made the apology I required,

XXIII.

The position of the army in front of Chattanooga was not as strong as we supposed, and the enemy succeeded in re-opening their communications and obtaining supplies. There was no longer any expectation that we should be able to starve them out, and it was determined to make a diversion in another direction. The plan was to detach Longstreet, who should pass down the Sweet Water Valley and capture Burnside's forces which were in the neighbor-hood of Knoxville. Before going away, I was exceedingly anxious to complete the equipment of our corps, but Bragg's Chief of Ordnance, Colonel Oladowski, was in-ordinately fond of red tape, and I should have been in bad plight but for a quantity of Enfield rifles I had prudently brought from Virginia with me. Oladowski could outcurse any man in the army I ever met, except Jubal Early and M. W. Gary. It was one of his boasts that he had "evacuate Murphreysboro' with zee whole army and lose only one grindstone." It disgusted him, too, that Colonel Manning should have been wounded. He said to me: "My friend! what for Colonel Manning he go into zee fight?" I told him it was the custom of our Ordnance officers to do so. " I tell you sar," said Oladowski, "he not go into zee fight for love zee country. I know! I know! he go into zee fight to get promotion and zee little furlough. Vell! vell! vell! I wish I was in h—ll ten year before dis war begin!"

I learned afterwards that Oladowski was the Ordnance Sergeant at the Baton Rouge Arsenal at the time the war began, and, of course not a man of education or position.

He was a good-hearted fellow, but I fear that after the disastrous defeat of Bragg's army at the battle of Missionary Ridge, after Longstreet's departure, he could not well have congratulated himself on having lost "only one grindstone."

Early in November we left Chattanooga, and marched by the Sweet Water Valley and Loudon to Knoxville. One of General Longstreet's most serious faults as a military commander was shown at this time. To his knowledge we were to cut loose from our communications, with no certainty that we should soon be able to re-establish them. It would indeed be easy enough to live upon the country, but we could not hope to find in the fields or the corn-cribs either small-arm or artillery ammunition. Nevertheless, he gave me no notice whatever that any extended movement was to be made, nor did he warn me that I must be prepared to supply the army with ammunition for the campaign. Not one word was said to me by him on the subject. I had an inkling, however, of what was going on, and obtained ample supplies. Had I not done so, we should have been in an awkward predicament by the time that we reached Knoxville. Had anything been lacking, it is certain that the blame would have been placed on me. It is evident that it was Longstreet's duty, as a prudent commander, to confer with the chiefs of the several staff departments, ascertain from them what was the condition of their supplies, and inform them what was likely to be required. If he had not such confidence in them as would permit him to give them the necessary information, he should have removed them and put in their places officers whom he could trust. It is certain that he could have given the requisite instructions without divulging the details of the movement.

14

At Loudon we found that the enemy had destroyed the bridge across the Tennessee River and had smashed some locomotives and cars which had been left there. The process was very simple. The trains were made up, and when there was a full head of steam the throttles of the locomotives were opened, and they were allowed to whirl along the track until they reached the parapet of the bridge, whence they bounded into the river below.

Crossing the river on an unstable pontoon bridge, we found ourselves within striking distance of Burnside's Corps at Lenoir Station. For two days there was sharp fighting with the enemy's rear guard. Then our opportunity came. McLaws was ordered to press on to Campbell's Station, while Hood's Division, under Jenkins, took the road which follows the line of the railroad to Lenoir Station. Jenkins made a vigorous advance, and Burnside found it impracticable to move all his artillery and wagons. Some hundred of the latter, loaded with subsistence stores, ammunition and implements, were disabled and abandoned. The cannon powder lay on the ground four or five inches deep. It was a pleasant place where to smoke a quiet pipe, and several of my men indulged themselves in that way to my great discomfort. The expectation was that McLaws would reach the intersecting road in time to cut off Burnside, but McLaws was behind time, as usual, and we did not bag our game. General Sam Jones has just published an account of the Knoxville campaign, and I give here what he says about the failure to intercept Burnside:

The march on the 16th was a race for position, but a slow one, because of the condition of the roads. McLaws was ordered to march as rapidly as possible to the intersection of the road on which he was marching with that which Jenkins was following, in the hope of reaching it before the Federals. General Longstreet was eager to force his adversary to accept battle, and General Burnside just as eager to avoid it until he could reach Knoxville.

The distance from Lenoir to Campbell's Station is about eleven miles. Jenkins' instructions were to press the enemy vigorously and do his utmost to bring him to bay. The advance and rear guards were several times hotly engaged, the latter halting only long enough to cover the retreat and then following. About 11 o'clock Jenkins' division reached the junction of the two roads about a mile from Campbell's Station. McLaws' Division had not arrived, and the Federals had passed it.

General McLaws' orders were to move rapidly to Campbell's Station and endeavor to reach that point before the Federals. His march during this day, the 16th, was as rapid as the condition of the roads would permit, and not materially retarded by the troops that General Hartranft had sent forward for the purpose, a small body of Colonel Hart's cavalry keeping back the enemy's skirmisher's with but slight loss. By the time McLaws reached the vicinity of Campbell's Station the Federals had been so closely pressed by Hood's Division as to be obliged to face about and form line of battle, which they did about a mile from the station. When McLaws arrived he was ordered to deploy three of his brigades in front of the enemy and to put his other brigade (Humphrey's) upon a ridge on his left, to threaten the enemy's right, but not to show his division beyond the woods skirting the plain towards Campbell's Station. Colonel Alexander placed his artillery in position and General Jenkins ordered three of his brigades, McLaws' and Anderson's, supported by Benning's, around the enemy's left flank, the movement being concealed by a wooded ridge, with instructions to attack vigorously. McLaws was to attack in front when he should hear Jenkins' guns.

This flank movement, which did not escape the vigilance of the Federals, caused them to fall back, a rather difficult and hazardous move to make in the face of an enemy. McLaws' Division advanced promptly and brought them to a stand in their second and stronger position, about a mile further towards Knoxville. The ground over which McLaws' and Anderson's Brigades had to move to strike the enemy's left and rear was very rough ; over steep hills covered with a thick growth of scrub oak, which necessarily delayed them, while they were exposed to the fire of the enemy's artillery. Before McLaws', Benning's and Anderson's Brigades reached the left of the enemy's position that position had been abandoned for the second and stronger one.

General Longstreet earnestly desired a general engagement and did his utmost to compel his adversary to accept it before reaching Knoxville, rightly judging, it would seem, that to do so offered the best prospect for the success of his expedition. The opportunity was offered at Campbell's Station. General Burnside was forced to halt there and form line of battle to cover his trains, which obstructed the road by which he was retreating. He held his position there six or seven hours, but before the Confederates could be placed in position night came on so dark and rainy that the attack could not be made. Ably seconded by his officers and the steadiness of his troops he skilfully extricated his command from a perilous position.

" If," says General Longstreet, " General Jenkins could have made his attack during this movement (the withdrawal from the first to the second position) or if he could have made it after the enemy had taken his second position, we must have destroyed this force, recovered East Tennessee, and in all probability captured the greater part of the enemy's forces." When such an opportunity is lost in a campaign blame is generally attached to some one or more commanders; and this was not an exception to the general rule. But when the weather and the condition of the roads is considered it is not surprising that their movements were not as rapid as could have been wished. The weather was most unfavorable ; frequent rains, especially on the 13th and 14th, had rendered the steep and rugged roads almost impassable for artillery and wagons.

XXIV.

Burnside fell back to Knoxville, and we went into camp around the town. The principal defensive work was Fort Sanders, which had walls twenty feet high, with a ditch ten feet deep. Efforts were made to guard the river, both below and above Knoxville, so as to prevent Burnside from receiving supplies or reinforcements, and the works were occasionally shelled. There was a good deal of delay, for one reason and another, and we were so near the town that we could hear the tunes played by the band at Fort Sanders. The favorite air then was: "When this Cruel War is Over." Finally, an attack was ordered to be made on Fort Sanders, but, although our men fought with their usual gallantry, they were driven back. This was on the 29th of November. In front of the fort trees had been cut, so as to fall with their branches outward, and wires had been stretched from stump to stump to trip up any assailants. Our men struggled through the abattis under a deadly fire, and some of them crossed the ditch and climbed up the parapet, but they were hurled back by the defenders of the fort, and thrown into the ditch. Hand grenades were used by the garrison with great effect. A second assault was tried, but equally in vain. These attacks cost us about five hundred men.

In one of the attacks we made, Captain Winthrop, of the 44th Foot, in the English army, who was on leave of absence, and had been with us for some time, behaved with the most brilliant gallantry. We were taking a hasty lunch in the breastworks under fire as the assault began, and Winthrop rode off to see what was going on. Finding that the troops were advancing, he rode out in front of the line and right up to the enemy's works, striking with his sword at the soldiers who held them. In less time than it takes to tell it he was lying on the ground with a big hole in his collar bone. It was a very painful wound, but he recovered.

The attack on Knoxville having failed utterly, and tidings having been received of the defeat of Bragg, at Missionary Ridge, Longstreet raised the siege, and retreated to Virginia. The rest of the winter we passed on the line of railroad between Knoxville and Bristol, my head-quarters being at Russellville. The men suffered frightfully. It is no exaggeration to say that on such marches as they were obliged to make in that bitter weather they left the bloody tracks of their feet on the sharp stones of the roads.

It was a bleak, desolate, inhospitable country, yet we managed to have a merry Christmas, although there was considerable difficulty in getting the requisite quantum of brandy to make egg-nog with. The medical staff had plenty of whiskey and brandy, for the sick and wounded, and a good deal of the stimulants went, I am sure, to those who did not require them. There were some stills in the neighborhood, and there was active demand for all the liquor these could supply. I have known our people to fill their canteens with the apple jack, as it dropped from the end of the worm, and drink it delightedly, as soon as by immersing the canteen in a branch they had cooled the liquor sufficiently to allow it to be gulped down. I sent Henry Tyler on Christmas Eve to a place ten or fifteen miles away to get a canteen of apple jack for our Christmas egg-nog. Morning came, and he did not return. We were very uneasy, as the woods were the favorite lurking place of bushwhackers. As one of my men explained, "there was a whacker in every bush." In the

middle of the day Tyler turned up. Overcome by the cold
or fatigue, he had gone to sleep in the middle of the road,
and when he awoke in the morning he found an empty canteen by his side, and his horse standing a few paces off.
But it was a hard winter, in spite of egg-nog and apple jack.

Finding that there was no probability of an early move,
I asked permission to go down to Richmond for a few days.
Leave was given me, but I had to ride about sixty miles in
intensely cold weather, on a fiendishly obstinate and per-
verse mule, to reach Bristol, where I took the cars for
Richmond. By this time Confederate soldiers were treated
with scant respect by the railroad officials. On our way to
the Sweet Water Valley, I remember the conductor quietly
stopped the train and told us that we should not go on,
unless we cut a supply of wood for his engine. But it was
worse on the train that was to take us to Lynchburg.
There was no fire in the cars at night, and I really thought
I should have frozen. The men in the cars stood it as long
as they could, and, when they found that the conductor
would do nothing for them, they deliberately broke up the
blinds of the car, and with these made a fire which furnished
sufficient warmth to keep us from freezing. Had the conductor resisted, I believe the indignant Confederates would
have killed him; and in that case a jury of soldiers, at all
events, would have returned a verdict of justifiable homicide.

While at Mr. Tyler's, at Richmond, I found that I had
been recommended very strongly for promotion to the
rank of Captain; but was informed that it was necessary
that I should stand an examination before the recommendation could be complied with. It seemed rather an absurd
thing that I should be required to be examined, when General Longstreet and Colonel Baldwin, the Chief Ordnance

officer of General Lee's army, had shown by their recommendations that I was fully qualified for the duties that I had to discharge. So I went to Mr. Seddon, the Secretary of War, and told him what I thought of it. Kind old man as he was, he listened to me very patiently when I explained to him that I had been too long in the field to know as much as a youngster who had just been graduated from college, and that if my promotion depended upon my familiarity with Conic Sections and the Calculus, I should probably remain a Lieutenant all my life. Mr. Seddon said it was necessary to undergo an examination, but he would make an endorsement upon the papers that would put me in a proper position. The endorsement was this: "The Board, in examining Lieutenant Dawson for promotion, will make due allowance for any deficiency in theoretical knowledge which may have been caused by the engrossing nature of his duties in the field."

When I returned to head-quarters, I found that Colonel Manning had recovered; and a Board, consisting of Manning and two Captains of Artillery, was appointed to examine me. The examination was both written and oral. I was to answer in writing certain questions which had been sent from Richmond, and was then to be examined by the members of the Board. The written examination was rather wide in its scope, as it ranged from questions so simple as: "What is the centre of gravity?" and "What is a logarithm?" to such a question as this: "With a gun of a given calibre and at a given elevation, and with a given charge of powder and a projectile of a given weight, what will be the velocity of the projectile as it passes the muzzle of the piece?" My answer to some such question as this was: "I don't know." The oral examination was very funny, as Colonel Manning insisted that the calibre of a 10 pound Parrott was three inches, although I assured him it was only two and nine-tenths. As may be imagined, taking Colonel Manning's lack of familiarity with Ordnance duty into account and the suggestive endorsement of the Secretary of War, I passed my examination with flying colors.

Colonel Manning was taken ill and obliged to leave us for a time, and there was no event of importance, except a change in my head-quarters from Russellville to Abingdon, until April, 1864, when we were ordered to Gordonsville. On our way there I stopped to see Colonel Manning, who was being taken care of at a private house at Charlottesville, and to my great joy received from him my commission as Captain of Artillery, dated April 2d, 1864.

15

XXV.

On May 4th, Grant crossed the Rapidan, and the Wilderness Campaign began. General Lee put his troops in motion, and the next morning Ewell attacked Warren's Corps. Grant immediately ordered Hancock to attack A. P. Hill, and the battle raged until night. The fight was renewed the next morning, when Hill was driven back in some confusion. It was a critical moment for our army. Longstreet arrived in time to change the tide of battle. Kershaw's Division was in front, and the men were eager to show their old comrades that they had not become demoralized in the West. Without a pause, they formed in line of battle, arrested the enemy's advance, and drove him rapidly back. General Lee put himself at the head of the troops to conduct the attack in person, but the men swarmed around him, telling him, with tears in their eyes, that he must go back, and that if he would go back they would make short work of the enemy. Everything went well with us for some time. General Longstreet ascertained that the left of the enemy's line extended but a short distance beyond the Plank-road, and Lieutenant-Colonel Sorrell, the Adjutant-General of Longstreet's Corps, was sent to conduct the brigades of Mahone, G. T. Anderson and Wofford around the enemy's left, and attack him on his left and rear. They did this with perfect success, and the enemy fell back with heavy loss to a position about three-quarters of a mile from our front. It was the moment to make a bold stroke for victory. The whole of Longstreet's Corps, with R. H. Anderson's Division, was to be thrown *en masse* against the staggering enemy. Longstreet, with

Colonel Sorrel, Captain Manning, of the Signal Corps, and myself, with some couriers, rode down the Plank-road at the head of our column. Just then, General Jenkins, who commanded a South Carolina brigade in our corps, rode up, his face flushed with joy, and, shaking hands with Longstreet, congratulated him on the result of the fight. Turning then to his brigade, which was formed in the road, Jenkins said: "Why do you not cheer, men?" The men cheered lustily, and hardly had the sound died away when a withering fire was poured in upon us from the woods on our right. Jenkins, rising in his stirrups, shouted out: "Steady, men! For God's sake, steady!" and fell mortally wounded from his saddle. Longstreet, who had stood there like a lion at bay, reeled as the blood poured down over his breast, and was evidently badly hurt. Two of General Jenkins' staff were killed by the same volley. What others thought I know not. My own conviction was that we had ridden into the midst of the enemy, and that nothing remained but to sell our lives dearly. The firing ended as suddenly as it began, and we then learned that Longstreet had been wounded and Jenkins had been killed, as Jackson was, by the fire of our own men. It was but the work of a few minutes. We lifted Longstreet from the saddle, and laid him on the side of the road. It seemed that he had not many minutes to live. My next thought was to obtain a surgeon, and, hurriedly mentioning my purpose, I mounted my horse and rode in desperate haste to the nearest field hospital. Giving the sad news to the first surgeon I could find, I made him jump on my horse, and bade him, for Heaven's sake, ride as rapidly as he could to the front where Longstreet was. I followed afoot. The flow of blood was speedily staunched, and Longstreet was placed in an ambulance. Poor Jenkins also received every attention, but remained insensible until he died.

The disaster which had befallen us arrested for a time the movement of the troops, for none but Longstreet knew what General Lee's intentions were. Sadly riding back, surrounding the ambulance, we met General Lee, and I shall not soon forget the sadness in his face, and the almost despairing movement of his hands, when he was told that Longstreet had fallen. It was a few minutes after twelve o'clock when Longstreet was hit, and General C. W. Field, the ranking Division Commander, took command of the corps. It was four o'clock when the attack was made. By this time, the shattered lines in our front had been restored, and our movement was unsuccessful. It seemed a fatality that our onslaught should have been arrested at the moment when the promise of victory was brightest. So ended the Battle of the Wilderness, May 6, 1864.

The next day I ascertained how the sad accident had happened. The woods are very dense in the Wilderness, and the dust was so thick as to reduce every tree and shrub to one uniform shade of gray. Mahone's Brigade, which had formed part of the flanking column, was drawn up parallel with the Plank-road, and about sixty yards from it. The 6th Virginia became detached from the regiments on its right or left, and lost its position in the woods. When the 6th Virginia, isolated as it was, heard the cheering in front, the men supposed that the enemy were upon them. Without orders one soldier discharged his piece, and a volley was then fired by the whole line, with the mournful result I have described.

General R. H. Anderson was now placed in command of the corps, and with him my relations were pleasant from the beginning. Indeed, we became close friends.

XXVI.

From the Wilderness the army moved parallel with Grant to Spotsylvania Court House, where we had some desperate fighting. My usual good luck followed me, and I came no nearer being hit than having a solid shot strike the place where my feet had been resting a moment before.

Baffling Grant completely at Cold Harbor, and forcing him to abandon the line on which he had promised to "fight it out if it took all summer," we found ourselves, early in June, on our way to Petersburg, crossing the river at Drury's Bluff. We had with us the divisions of Pickett and of Field, and were to move down the Turnpike towards Petersburg, to occupy the lines from which General Beauregard had withdrawn. This was on June 16th. It was a delightful day, and General Anderson and his staff rode on a considerable distance in advance of the troops. There was no more expectation of encountering the enemy than we should have of finding him in the streets of Charleston. When we neared Chester, however, a Major Smith, who was in haste to reach Petersburg, and had gone on ahead, came tearing back "bloody with spurring and fiery red with haste," and without his hat. We were at a loss to understand what this meant, and he had not breath enough left to tell us at the moment. As soon as he could speak, he said that near the point where the railroad crossed the Turnpike he had seen the Yankees in the woods as thick as bees; and a party of them was then engaged in tearing up the line of railroad which formed the only means of communication between the Confederate capital and Petersburg. He was fired at, but his horse alone was hit; and it was a lucky escape for us. Had we jogged on very much farther we should have found ourselves in the hands of the enemy, who, it seems, had pushed up from Bermuda Hundreds, on finding that the lines in front of them had been vacated, and were about to make good their occupation of the railroad. We halted in the road until the leading regiment of our column came up, when it was deployed in the woods, and advanced until it struck the enemy. The next day an effort was made to recover our lost line ; and on the 18th Pickett took it with a rush. Kershaw had gone on to Petersburg. There we had our head-quarters until near the end of June.

Petersburg had changed very much from the quiet, peaceful, drowsy looking city it was when I first knew it. But it was an agreeable place to be in, for one reason at least. During the Wilderness campaign our rations had been reduced to five ounces of bacon and twelve ounces of corn meal daily, and the country was so bare that no additions could be made to our scant fare. At Richmond and Petersburg there was little difficulty in obtaining provisions of every kind, the joke being, however, that housekeepers took their money to market in a basket and brought home in their pockets what they had bought for dinner.

The Petersburgers had accommodated themselves to the changed conditions with curious completeness. Shell frequently fell in or passed over the city, and it was no uncommon thing for old citizens, standing in the street discussing the prospects of the day, to step quietly around a corner until an approaching shell had passed by, and then resume their former place without even suspending their conversation. The basements of houses were used in many instances as bomb-proofs, the traverses being composed of mattresses and bedding.

From Petersburg we went back to the North side of the

James River, and on July 28th captured a piece of artillery and some prisoners near the Long Bridge Road.

Early in August General Anderson was summoned to Richmond for consultation with President Davis and General Lee; and on August 7th we took the train for Mitchell Station, where Kershaw's Division soon arrived, and three days later Fitz Lee's Cavalry Division came up.

I should mention here that my friend Mr. Raines had suffered a terrible loss. The enemy made a raid through Sussex County and carried off a number of his negroes and nearly the whole of his horses and mules. Fortunately, the raiders feared that they might be cut off if they took the road by Belsches' Mill-pond to the Plank-road, and they did not pass by Mr. Raines' residence, which, therefore, was not destroyed. One of my riding horses which I valued very highly was carried off by the cavalry. Mr. Raines and his family were not at home at the time, having gone to Mechlenburg County, where his son-in-law, Dr. Wm. H. Jones, resided. While I was at Petersburg I became very unwell, and our Medical Director, Dr. Cullin, told me that there was only one prescription that he knew of that would cure me quickly, and that was a leave of absence. Leave for fifteen days was given me, and I started off in an ambulance to Sussex. When I reached there I found old Davie, the butler (a counterpart of our own Levy, although considerably older), in charge of the place, and the family absent. This did not daunt me, although I was sadly disappointed. I hired a buggy and went on to Mechlenburg. The plantation of Dr. Jones was near Boydton, and I remained there about two weeks. The family consisted then of Dr. Jones and his wife, the eldest daughter of Mr. Raines, and their little daughter Anna; with Miss Anna

Raines and Miss Patty Raines, the daughters of my old friend; and Frank and Nat, his sons. Miss Pinkie Morton and Miss Hattie Morton, nieces of Dr. Jones, and his wards, were also there. The plantation was large and valuable, the principal crop made on it being tobacco of a fine quality. I found at the plantation a thoroughbred Belshazzar colt, which I had bought in Tennessee; a fancy looking cream-colored animal, with a long mane and tail, of which I expected great things. His career was brief, and not particularly glorious. When the Yankees made a raid through Boydton, after General Lee's surrender, they visited Dr. Jones' house and carried off my Belshazzar colt. He was loose in the pasture, and they had considerable difficulty in catching him, as he jumped over the fence whenever they got him in a corner. It was only by surrounding him that they caught him at last.

The conduct of the Yankees at Dr. Jones' was infamous in the extreme. Mrs. Jones was on her death-bed, but the soldiers, after tying Dr. Jones and putting him under guard, forced themselves into her bed-room, and there in her presence broke open her bureau and carried off what valuables they could find. It was well that they did no worse.

The object of our expedition to the Valley, to which I now return, I have never thoroughly understood, but I presume that it was to act in concert with General Early, and do what mischief we could. From Mitchell Station we moved through Culpepper and Flint Hill to Front Royal. The weather was so beautiful that it was hard to believe that we had any serious business before us. An effort was made to obstruct our passage of the Shenandoah, a river which is aptly named, if ever river was. With its clear waters dancing and sparkling in the autumn sun, it deserved its title as "Fair Daughter of the Stars." Wofford's Brigade was sent forward to attack the enemy's cavalry, and, according to our joke at head-quarters, "Wofford swung his right and made a water-haul." Seriously, he was charged by the enemy, who had driven back our own cavalry, and was compelled to retire with heavy loss. I think that his Ordnance officer was among the killed.

The enemy withdrew, and from Front Royal we marched down the Valley in pursuit. I then realized, as never before, the devastation of war. Columns of smoke were rising in every direction from burning houses and burning barns. Each time that we lighted our pipes that day, it was with the burning embers taken from the ruins of what a few hours before had been a happy home. The brutal Sheridan was carrying out his fell purpose, and was soon in position to boast, ruthless braggart as he is! that "If a crow wants now to fly over the Valley of Virginia, he must carry his rations with him." It was the penalty that the Virginians of the Valley paid for their devotion to the Confederacy, and, despite their fearful losses, the time never came when a Confederate soldier could not obtain a crust of bread from any Southern family there. They always contrived to have something left, and whatever they had they were ready to share with the ragged and hungry Confederates.

On the march, by the way, there was an exciting incident. General Anderson, with the staff and couriers, was far ahead of the infantry column, and we had a squadron of cavalry as our escort and advance guard. A couple of shots were suddenly fired, and in an instant our cavalry broke and came clattering to the rear. The indignation of General Anderson was painful to see. He cried out to our

16

cavalry: "What manner of men do you call yourselves," and putting his hand involuntarily to his side, said: "Oh, if I had my sabre!" Turning to his staff and couriers, he said: "Charge those people in front," pointing to the blue-coated cavalry, who were as much astonished at coming upon us as we were at meeting with them. It was a mutual surprise. The staff with the couriers dashed at the handful of cavalry who had driven in our advance guard, and we had a glorious race down the Turnpike to the suburbs of Winchester. I think we captured four or five Yankees, without any loss on our side, and my share of the plunder was a very good McClellan saddle and a small sum in greenbacks. It was only fair, I suppose, that we should confiscate the greenbacks which we found in the possession of the men we captured, as we expected them to take possession of what money we had whenever we were captured. It is true that Confederate money was not likely to be as useful to them as greenbacks were to us, but it would not have been patriotic to make any distinction between the two currencies. I had paid $5 in Richmond for blacking my boots, and the negro who performed the office would have felt himself well paid if I could have given him instead a ten cent Yankee shin-plaster.

Near Charlestown, on August 26th, the enemy felt our position to some purpose, and captured about one hundred men belonging to the 15th South Carolina Regiment, of Kershaw's Brigade. Then we marched and counter-marched and danced about in every direction, with no definite object apparently, until September 3d, when we moved out from Winchester, and attacked the enemy near Berryville, and drove him away. It was at this time that the whole command could have been gobbled up. We had only Kershaw's

Division with us, the cavalry having been sent off on a re-connoissance. The enemy, in overwhelming force, came upon us, and General Anderson reached the conclusion that nothing but audacity would save us. Presenting as bold a front as if the whole of the Army of Northern Virginia were with us, and bringing our wagon trains right up to the line of battle, he opened on the enemy with our artillery. To our great surprise and relief the game was successful, and the enemy drew off. General Early arrived the next morning, and his first salutation was: "General Anderson, those Yankees came mighty near getting you yesterday." General Anderson's only reply was: "Yes General, and it is not your fault that they did not." It was a strange business anyway. General Anderson ranked General Early, but did not wish to take command of his troops, as he would necessarily have done had the two commands operated together. The result was that the two commands swung corners and chasséed in every direction to no good purpose, that any of us could see. It was a delightful sort of military pic-nic, and in that sense everybody enjoyed it.

In September we were ordered back to Culpepper, and the march through the Luray Valley, in delicious weather, put us in excellent spirits. General Anderson said to me one morning, looking up at the blue peaks which were frowning down upon us, that it would be the heighth of happiness, for him, to lie on the top of one of those mountains all day long and roll rocks down its rugged sides.

The day before we reached Culpepper I found myself very nearly afoot. Two of my horses were missing, and so was my servant, Aleck. This boy had been with me from the time that I returned from Fort Delaware, and was as faithful a servant as one could desire to have. He had charge of my clothes, and generally kept my purse. No one could have been more conscientious and trustworthy than he appeared to be; but he was gone this time, and so were the horses. Taking one of the couriers, an Alabamian, named Spencer (who was afterwards appointed Aide-de-Camp to Colonel Sorrell, when that officer was promoted to the rank of Brigadier-General), I rode back in pursuit of the runaway. For two days and nights we kept on his trail, but were unable to overtake him, and as we were uncomfortably near the main body of the enemy's troops, we returned to Culpepper, finding that our people had reached that place just in time to drive off a raiding party which had pounced down upon the village. Long afterwards I met Aleck in Petersburg, and asked him what he meant by stealing my horses. He grinned and said: "Mas'r Frank, I didn't go for teef dem horse, but dere was a gal back dere in Winchester I was bound to see, and when I git dere de Yankee tek my horse and I couldn't git away again." This excuse served as well as any would have done.

Kershaw's Division was sent back to reinforce Early, and we went on to Richmond and thence to Swift Run, between Richmond and Petersburg.

XXVII.

General Anderson's first visit was to General R. E. Lee, who was at dinner, and insisted on our dining with him. It was the most uncomfortable meal that I ever had in my life. General Lee was fond of quizzing young officers, and my frame of mind can be imagined when General Lee spoke to me in this way: "Mr. Dawson, will you take some of this bacon? I fear that it is not very good, but I trust that you will excuse that. John! give Mr. Dawson some water; I pray pardon me for giving you this cup. Our table service is not as complete as it should be. May I give you some bread? I fear it is not well baked, but I hope you will not mind that," &c., &c., &c.; while my cheeks were red and my ears were tingling, and I wished myself anywhere else than at General Lee's head-quarters.

On September 28th, General Anderson was ordered to move to the North side of the James River and assume command there. Early the next morning he and his staff and couriers set out for Chaffin's Bluff. We had ridden some miles when a courier came up in a condition of desperate excitement, and told us that the enemy in great force had attacked the works on the North side of the river, near Chaffin's Bluff, had captured Battery Harrison, and were probably by this time in Richmond. Sending him on to General Lee's head-quarters, we put spurs to our horses and rode at a gallop to the river, where we crossed the pontoon bridge and found the condition of affairs almost as bad as had been described. Nothing but want of dash on the part of the enemy had prevented them from taking Richmond. The lines had been held by four or five hundred men of our command, with a small number of the Home Guard from Richmond, and when the enemy had taken Battery Harrison the roads were open to them and they had nothing to do but march right into the Confederate Capital. Fortunately for us, they believed us to be much stronger than we were and waited for reinforcements. Only one hundred and fifty men occupied Battery Harrison when it was attacked. In the afternoon Laws' Brigade came to our assistance, and with Gregg and Benning repulsed a desperate attack made by the enemy on Battery Gilmer. Here we saw that colored troops could be made to fight for one dash at all events. They came right up to the fort very resolutely, but, encountering an obstinate resistance, they gave way completely and took refuge in the ditch, where they were easily disposed of. It was just the sort of fight that any one would like. Shells with the fuses cut to a half second were thrown into the ditch and played havoc with the terror-stricken negroes.

The next morning, September 30th, General Lee having obtained reinforcements, an effort was made to retake Battery Harrison. The attack was not well arranged apparently, and failed completely. A new defensive line was therefore taken up and fortified, and the enemy were left to make the most of their barren conquest.

There was no fighting of much importance after this until October 7th, when we made an attempt to turn the enemy's right and drive him back to the river. At first the movement was completely successful and we captured nine pieces of artillery and some prisoners, but when we struck the enemy in position near the New Market Road we were repulsed and General Gregg was killed. It was on this day, unless I am mistaken, that, in a cavalry charge, Colonel A.

C. Haskell, of the Seventh, S. C. Cavalry, was desperately wounded, and for a time in the hands of the enemy. Volunteers were called for to make a charge and recover the body, and one of these volunteers was C. S. McCall, of Bennettsville, who is now State Senator from Marlboro' County, in this State, and as gallant a soldier and as good a fellow as we had in the army. There was a touching incident this day when Gregg's Brigade had been repulsed and Gregg had fallen mortally wounded. General Lee, with General Anderson and a number of officers, was watching the attack, when a boy apparently about eighteen or nineteen years old, his uniform dabbled with blood and his arms hanging limp by his sides, came up to General Lee, and nodding to him said: "General! if you don't send some more men down there, our boys will get hurt sure." General Lee asked him if he was wounded. "Yes, sir," he replied. "Where are you wounded?" asked General Lee. "I am shot through both arms, General; but I don't mind that General! I want you to send some more men down there to help our boys." General Lee told him that he would attend to it, and directed one of his staff officers to take charge of this poor boy and see that he was properly cared for.

In a letter which I wrote to England about this time, I gave the price of different articles in Confederate money: a pair of cavalry boots $350; coffee $15 a pound; sugar $10 a pound; a linen collar $5; a pocket handkerchief $10; Richmond papers 50 cents each; tobacco, which two years before was 25 and 30 cents a pound, was selling at $8 or $9 a pound. For the making of a pair of trowsers I paid $100.

XXVIII.

A sudden and very welcome change in my position now took place. I cannot say that my connection with General Longstreet had been pleasant to me personally, for the reason that he was disposed to be reserved himself, while the principal members of his staff, with two exceptions, were positively disagreeable. Colonel Sorrell, the Adjutant-General, was bad tempered and inclined to be overbearing. Colonel Fairfax was clownish and silly, and Major Walton, whom I have mentioned before, was always supercilious. Colonel Osman Latrobe was courteous enough at all times, and Colonel Manning was exceedingly kind and considerate. Besides Colonel Manning, I had not a friend on the staff. The staff had "no use" for me, which was perhaps not surprising, as I was a stranger and a foreigner, and I was on no better terms with them in 1864 than I had been in 1862. Still I had the satisfaction of knowing that I had a good reputation in the army as an officer, and that it was known at General Lee's head-quarters that the whole responsibility in the Ordnance Department of the corps rested upon me. General Anderson had been promoted to the rank of Lieutenant-General, and was to take command of a corps at Petersburg when General Longstreet should return to duty, and he was kind enough to tell me that if Colonel Baldwin, the Chief of Ordnance of the army, would consent to the transfer, he would take me with him to Petersburg, and make me Chief Ordnance Officer of his corps. This would have given me the rank of Major or Lieutenant-Colonel. I rode over to Petersburg to see Colonel Baldwin, and he told me that he would be delighted to see me promoted, and would order the assignment to be made. Unfortunately, though properly, General Anderson, upon reflection, came to the conclusion that it would not be just to Captain E. N. Thurston, who had been his Ordnance Officer while he was in command of a division, to promote me over his head, and that he ought to make Captain Thurston his Chief Ordnance Officer. I assented, of course, but was determined to seize any opportunity that offered to leave Longstreet's Corps. As far back, indeed, as the month of June I had made a written application to be relieved from duty with the command. The opportunity came when I least expected it. General Fitzhugh Lee, a nephew of General R. E. Lee, while in the command of the cavalry in the Valley of Virginia had lost his Ordnance Officer, Captain Isaac Walke, of Norfolk, Virginia, who was killed in action, to the deep regret of his comrades. Through some kind friend General Lee heard of me. It seems that he had told Colonel Baldwin and others that he wanted an officer to take Captain Walke's place, who was both "a good officer and a gentleman." To my great pleasure I was recommended to him. He made application for me, and I was relieved from duty with Longstreet's Corps and directed to report to General Fitz Lee at Richmond. This was in November, 1864.

General Longstreet had already resumed command of the 1st Corps, and I have not seen him since I took leave of him before I went to join Fitz Lee. The reputation that Longstreet had as a fighting man was unquestionably deserved, and when in action there was no lack of energy or of quickness of perception, but he was somewhat sluggish by nature, and I saw nothing in him at any time to make me believe that his capacity went beyond the power to conduct a square hard fight. The power of combination he did not possess,

17

and whenever he had an independent command he was unsuccessful. A better officer to execute a prescribed movement, and make such variations in it as the exigencies of the battle required, would be hard to find, but he needed always a superior mind to plan the campaign and fix the order of battle. It should be said of Longstreet, especially in view of his political course since the war, that he never faltered or hesitated in his devotion to the Confederate cause. A stauncher soldier the South did not have, and at Appomattox, when hope was gone, and General Lee, to prevent the useless loss of blood, was prepared to surrender, Longstreet pleaded for permission to take the remnant of his men and endeavor to cut his way through the surrounding enemy. But Longstreet was a soldier, and nothing else. Of the principles that underlay secession he knew nothing, and when we were defeated, and the war was over, he considered that might had made the North right, and that he could, without any impropriety, go over to the victors. The whirligig of time brought its revenges, however, when Longstreet, at the head of the Metropolitan Police in New Orleans, endeavoring to maintain, by armed force, the political supremacy of the "carpet-baggers," was confronted and routed by the old soldiers of his corps, whom he had again and again led to victory in Virginia. They spared him in remembrance of what he had been, but they drove his Metropolitan Police like rabbits before them.

I have come across a note written by Mr. Frank Vizetelly, of the *Illustrated London News*, in 1864, in response to enquiries of one of my relatives in London, where Mr. Vizetelly then was. I give what he says, as the testimony of one who knew me while I was with Longstreet. The note is as follows: "Will you tell your friend that I knew

Lieutenant Dawson very well indeed. He is Ordnance Officer to General Longstreet, and when I left the Confederacy, at the end of January, he was quite well. He is very much liked, and is a very good officer, and, I have no doubt, will make his way." I should like to quote here also what was said by the Richmond *Examiner*, in 1863, about the Englishmen then in the Confederacy:

ENGLISHMEN IN OUR SERVICE.

Wherever and whenever a war for freedom is given, there Englishmen will be found, not for glory only, but for the natural bull-dog love of fighting and the inborn British love of the just cause and the weak side. Thus we find on the side of Yankee tyranny but one Englishman, Sir Percy Wyndham, who has lately quitted the Lincolnites in disgust; while on our side we find Colonel Grenfell still firm in his affection for the Stars and Bars; Captain Byrne, who lost a leg at Manassas, and insists upon fighting through the war; Captain Gordon of A. P. Hill's staff, who acted so gallantly at Fredericksburg; and many others, in both our Army and Navy. Among these "others" the name of Lieutenant Dawson deserves mention. Lieutenant D., a youth of eighteen or nineteen, insisted on coming over in the *Nashville*. Captain Pegram's sense of duty would not permit him to receive him as a passenger, so he shipped before the mast as a common sailor, and in that capacity did his duty faithfully and manfully. Arrived in this city, he at once joined the Purcell Battery as a private, and was wounded in one of the battles on the Chickahominy. As soon as his wound was well, General Randolph very justly promoted him to a Lieutenancy, which post he continues to fill with distinction and credit to the service. We bid him and the rest of his Anglo-Confederate comrades God speed, good luck, and plenty of promotion, for they are sure to deserve it. And if they are disposed to settle down in Dixie, we have no objection to their forming an alliance with some of our pretty Southern girls.

XXIX.

It was on November 10, 1864, that General Fitz Lee applied for me, and in a letter written to my mother at the time I said that General Longstreet was very reluctant to give me up.   I must say that he did not show any particular interest in retaining me as long as no one else wanted me.   General Fitz Lee was in Richmond, having been wounded in the Valley.   I reported to him, and was then directed to go to Harrisonburg, Va., and report to General T. L. Rosser, who was then in command of General Lee's Division.   I found that the head-quarters were near Harrisonburg, and was made most cordially welcome there.   Lieutenant Charles Minnigerode, son of Dr. Minnigerode, of Richmond, was aide-de-camp to General Lee, and he and I took a great fancy to each other immediately.   The other officers of the staff were Major Robert M. Mason, Chief Quarter-master and acting Inspector-General of the Division; Major W. B. Warwick, of Richmond, Chief Commissary; Dr. Archie Randolph, Medical Director.   Major J. Du Gué Ferguson, of Charleston, the Adjutant-General of the Division, had been taken prisoner, and was not with the command. Major Bowie, the Inspector-General, had been wounded at Spotsylvania, and did not rejoin the division.   A better set of fellows than Fitz Lee's staff it would have been difficult to find.   They formed in truth, according to the old phrase, the military family of General Lee.   There was no bickering, no jealousy, no antagonism.   We lived together as though we were near relatives, and I have the fondest and truest affection for every one of them.   Major Mason is a first cousin of General Fitz Lee, and I have not seen him for several years. Archie Randolph I have not heard of since the war ended. Minnigerode was the last man wounded in the Army of Northern Virginia. He was struck near the spine by a rifle ball while riding along the lines to give the order to cease firing, when the last flag of truce had been displayed at Appomattox. For many months he was paralyzed, but he has now entirely recovered, and when I last heard of him he was living in New Orleans.

I found that it was no joke to organize the Ordnance Department of a couple of divisions of Confederate cavalry, but I adapted myself to circumstances, and, having some good assistants, was able to get everything in tolerably good order. We then set out on a raid into Hardy County, West Virginia, for the purpose of capturing horses and cattle. The command, under the leadership of General Rosser, had made a week or two before a very successful raid upon New Creek, on the Baltimore and Ohio Railroad. They had captured the place and brought off a vast quantity of stores of different descriptions. The present raid was not so eventful. I had not known what cold was before this. The snow lay on the ground a foot deep, and the wind was so keen and bitter that it was difficult to face it. For miles the road lay on a narrow ledge, the mountain rising like a wall on the right, while on the left there was a nearly perpendicular fall of six hundred feet to the Valley below, where a brook, held in icy chains, was shining in the sun. One slip would have sent horse and rider headlong to the bottom of the precipice. Through such scenes as this we rode for a week without any serious accident. Right in the midst of the mountains we came upon the charming residence of Mr. Cunningham, who was living in a manner that seemed entirely out of keeping with the wilderness around him. In his house there was every comfort, with many a luxury that in the Confederacy we had almost forgotten. Miss Annie Cunningham was one of the prettiest women I have ever seen, and became at once the centre of attraction with our young officers. With sleighing parties during the day and singing and dancing at night, our short stay in Hardy County was inexpressibly pleasant. After we left them, as the spokesman of the enamored staff, and not speaking in any sense for myself, I wrote a passionate epistle to Miss Annie, which was entrusted to one of our scouts for delivery. In it I put all the pretty phrases which were suggested by the occasion and the object. Unluckily for me, the note did not reach the fair Annie, but fell into the hands of the Yankees, and was published afterwards in one of the Baltimore papers as a specimen Confederate love letter.

There was a good deal of talk at head-quarters about Captain Charles Cavendish, who reported to General Fitz Lee for duty at, or about, the time that General J. E. B. Stuart was killed, at Yellow Tavern, and who was now absent on leave. Cavendish represented himself to be a cousin of the Duke of Devonshire, and said he held a commission in the 18th Hussars. I knew him quite well later on, and it is indubitable that he was a thorough soldier. General Fitz Lee told me that just when Cavendish reported to him the enemy were attacking in force, and one of our regiments was ordered to charge. Cavendish was well mounted and handsomely equipped, and asked General Lee's permission to go in with the regiment. This permission was at once given, and Cavendish rode off. Ten minutes later he returned with his saddle on his head, saying that "a blasted Yankee had fired at him from behind a tree and killed his horse." This was a fact. Cavendish, however, shot the Yankee. There was some things about Cavendish that our fellows could not understand. Riding through the woods one day, he tore the leg of his trousers, and a bare red leg was plainly visible. Minnigerode expressed his surprise at the sight, when Cavendish bluntly informed him that in England gentlemen never wore drawers. The matter was referred to me for decision, and I was unable to confirm what Cavendish had said. It is the fact, however, I think, that the privates and non-commissioned officers in the crack cavalry regiments in England wear nothing but the trousers, in order to secure a closer and better fit. Cavendish remained with us for some time, and in Richmond led a very wild life. As usual in such cases, he became short of money, and his drafts on his noble relatives in England were freely discounted. Cavendish went away, and the drafts came back dishonored. Inquiries were then made about him in England, and it was ascertained that he was most inappropriately named Short, and that he had been a corporal or sergeant in one of the English cavalry regiments. Cavendish was punctilious, however, in the discharge of his duties at our headquarters, and paid his mess bills as promptly as any one else.

XXX.

After our return from Hardy County, bringing with us a large drove of cattle, we established our head-quarters at a railroad station, eight or ten miles beyond Staunton. General Early was down the Valley, in the neighborhood of Harrisonburg, and a large body of the enemy's cavalry moved up to attack him. They expected to make a raid on Gordonsville, if they did not encounter Early. On the Monday before Christmas day, 1864, we moved out from camp with our division, and marched to Harrisonburg. It was desperately cold, and the sleet froze as it fell. My hat by the evening was as stiff as a board, and had a heavy fringe of icicles. The horses were slipping and sliding at every step, and the thirty miles seemed like fifty. We rested for a few hours at Harrisonburg, and General Rosser ascertained where the enemy's cavalry, under Custer, were to encamp for the night. At one o'clock in the morning we moved out again, the plan being to go by devious paths to the neighborhood of Custer's camp, and there attack him at daybreak. Our whole effective force did not exceed five or six hundred men. The march was conducted with great judgment, and a little before daybreak, with no alarm given, the division formed in the woods on the edge of the open fields where, surrounded by blazing fires of fence rails, Custer's troopers lay. The rattling of the sleet and the howling of the wind had effectually concealed our movements; but the men were almost stiff with cold, and it was hard to see how they would manage to handle their carbines or sabres. Just before daybreak the order to charge was given. I was with General Rosser at the head of the column, and I shall never forget the astonishment of the Yankee sentinel, who, as our horses came upon him like ghosts from the bosom of the darkness, fired his carbine in the air, and cried out : " My God, where do all those men come from!" It was a complete surprise, and in ten minutes, and with very small loss to ourselves, we had driven Custer and his entire command, consisting of about 2,000 men, out of their camp, and sent them whirling down the Valley. I was slightly wounded in the left leg, but not disabled from duty. Custer was in a farm house near by, and the story goes that, when he made his escape, he was in the condition that Cavendish would have been in, if he had lost his trousers entirely.

After the first dash, which, happily for us, accomplished what was desired, our men were very hard to hold. Had Custer attacked us, I do not think that we should have stopped short of Staunton. Expecting a counter charge, I tried, with General William H. Payne, ("Billy" Payne of the Black Horse Cavalry) to rally some of our men on the colors; but when I had gathered a dozen or two together, and started after some more, the first squad melted away into the woods. By common consent, the whole command withdrew. Custer had gone off one way, and our people had gone off quietly in the opposite direction. No one remained but General Rosser, Minnigerode, Mason, Archie Randolph and I. General Rosser suggested that we might as well go on after Custer, and see what he was doing, and we moved down the Turnpike, following Custer's rear-guard at a respectful distance.

Three or four hundred yards away, on our right, coming along a converging road, was a body of thirty or forty men. They had their oil-cloths on, and it was difficult to tell who they were; but I had an unpleasant conviction that they

18

were Yankees. We were approaching fast the forks of the road where we should meet them, and I ventured to suggest to General Rosser that they were not our men, but he insisted that they were not Yankees, and that, anyhow, we had better go on and see. So we went on. We were not more than a hundred yards away when the strangers halted, and were evidently preparing to fire. The imperturbable Rosser remarked very serenely: "Well, Dawson, you are right, those fellows are Yankees, but there are not many of them. Let's charge them." And we four did charge them; and, to our amazement and relief, the Yankees put spurs to their horses and galloped off down the Valley. As often happens in war, audacity had saved us. Nothing would have been easier than for those Yankees to have gathered us in, for we were half frozen, and our horses were worn out with hard riding.

We rode back to Harrisonburg, and having accomplished what was desired, and given General Early time to withdraw his wounded and stores, we retired to Staunton. There we were soon joined by General Fitz Lee.

Staunton is a hospitable place, and few days passed without an invitation to a dinner or a dancing party. I realized completely the delightful difference between my position with Longstreet, and my position with General Lee. By General Lee we were treated always as if we were his kinsmen, but, intimate and affectionate as our intercourse was, no one of us could ever forget the respect due to his rank. What we did for him, however, was just as much for love as it was for military duty.

From Staunton, we now moved to Waynesboro', where there was much merry-making, and Minnigerode fell in love again, and secured a provisional sweetheart. Soon we were hurried to Richmond to head off a raiding party of the enemy.

One way and another I saw a good deal of General Rosser, and to my mind, there were few officers in the service who had as much military genius as he had. Instinctively, he seemed to know what was best to do, and how to do it. It appeared almost impossible to tire him, or to break him down, and I have known him to ride day after day for a couple of weeks with a running wound in his leg. Had he had the unlimited command of horses and material that the cavalry Generals on the other side had, we should have known little peace in the Confederacy. Unfortunately, however, there was something lacking in Rosser's character, which I can best express, perhaps, by repeating a warning which was given me soon after I joined the command. It was this: One of my fellow officers said to me, " If Rosser gives you any order to deliver for the movements of troops in action, be careful to get that order in writing, and then, if anything goes wrong in consequence of the order, it cannot be said that the fault is yours."

XXXI.

We camped below Richmond, and I obtained leave of absence to go to Boydton for a few days, and from Boydton I crossed over into North Carolina to make a visit to a friend who was staying there. The Roanoke River was so high that the ferryman was unwilling to cross; but by the payment of $250 in Confederate money I succeeded in inducing him to take me over. It was a foolish performance, as the chances were ten to one that we should not be able to make a landing on the other side. From North Carolina I then went to Stony Creek, where I was told that our division was. This little railroad station, which had looked when I first saw it, in 1862, as if it were not visited by ten persons in a month, was now a busy military post, several thousand Confederates being encamped around it. Finding that I had been misinformed, I hurried by a circuitous route to Richmond, the enemy having possession of the railroad between Stony Creek and Petersburg. I reported for duty just as the division was on the march from Richmond. Through Powhatan County we rode, and, as ours was the first large body of troops that had passed through that happy place, the scenes of the early months of the war were repeated, to the satisfaction and surprise of our men. Ladies came out to the roadside with cakes and sandwiches and milk, and our people enjoyed themselves thoroughly. It is true that there were rather more of us than even the hospitable people of Powhatan could accommodate. The ladies there were very much in the plight of a good woman to whose house I went in the first Maryland campaign. I rode up to ask for a glass of water, and, before I had said what I wanted, was told that I really could not get break-fast, as there was nothing left in the house. The kind soul told me that she had made up her mind, when she heard that General Lee's army was coming, to give every one of his soldiers something to eat, and, when she had stripped the smoke-house bare, and used up every dust of meal, she was warned that only one division of the army had gone by. Then she gave up her generous purpose in something very much like despair.

This time we did not strike the enemy, as expected, and returned to Richmond, stopping for a day in Powhatan, at the house of Mr. Harris, the brother of Major Harris, who was Beauregard's Engineer Officer at Charleston, and who planned the more important defences around that City. From Richmond we rode to Petersburg, and General Fitz Lee was placed in command of the cavalry corps of the Army of Northern Virginia, consisting of three divisions.

XXXII.

The end was now very near. On March 30th, 1865, we dined at Mrs. Cameron's, in Petersburg, and rode out late in the evening to overtake the command, which had gone towards Five Forks. The greater part of the night we were in the saddle, and what rest I had was on a couple of fence rails in a corn field. It was raining heavily. Early in the morning of March 31, our line was formed at Five Forks, as it is called, a place where five roads meet. A blacksmith's shop that was there furnished, when pulled down, excellent material for a breast-work. One of our servants came up and made some coffee for us, and those who know how hot poor coffee, in a tin cup, can be, will understand what our feelings were when the cavalry of the enemy drove in our pickets just as we were about to enjoy the refreshing draught. We did not wait for the cavalry, and we took our coffee with us. Later in the morning the enemy, supported by infantry, attacked us in force. Our men were fighting dismounted, and at first were driven back in some confusion. General Payne was severely wounded, and I had just time to shake hands with him as he was taken to the rear. I did not see him again until the next year, when he was living quietly at his own home, at Warrenton. It was very difficult to rally the men. For the moment they were completely demoralized. One fellow whom I halted as he was running to the rear, and whom I threatened to shoot if he did not stop, looked up in my face in the most astonished manner, and, raising his carbine at an angle of forty-five degrees, fired it in the air, or at the tops of the pines, and resumed his flight. It made me laugh, angry as I was.

There was only one thing to do, and that was to order a charge all along the line. The bugles sounded, and the very men whom it had been impossible to stop a few minutes before turned and attacked the enemy with an impetuosity that bore everything before it. The difficulty was, indeed, to keep the men from going too far. Their blood was up; they were mortified that they should have been thrown into confusion; and there was much trouble in preventing them from running right in upon the main body of the enemy.

There was a pause now in the operations, and General Pickett had joined us with his division of infantry. My dear old friend, Willie Pegram, who was by this time Colonel of artillery, was there with a part of his battalion. It was a great happiness to me to clasp his true hand again. The next day he was slain—dying, as he had hoped and prayed that he might, when the last hope of the Confederacy was gone. This pure, sweet, brave man, a type of the unaffected Christian soldier, remained on his horse when the Federal infantry poured in over our works, and fell to the ground mortally wounded, at the very end of the fight. To Gordon McCabe, his Adjutant, who was with him then, he spoke his last words: " I have done what I could for my country, and now I turn to my God."

Towards evening a desperate charge was made by W. H. F. Lee's Division, in which we lost heavily. The movement was taken up by the divisions in the centre and on the left, and we broke the enemy's infantry and scattered them like chaff before us. I flattered myself that my usual good luck would attend me, for, as I rode abreast of the line and bowed my head in passing under a tree, the bough which I had stooped to escape was struck sharply by a rifle ball.

But only two or three minutes afterward I was shot squarely
in the arm, near the shoulder, and put *hors de combat*.
Archie Randolph was by me in a minute, and poured an
indefinite quantity of apple brandy down my throat. This
revived me, and, with my arm in a sling, I rode back to
where General Fitz Lee was, only to be ordered perempto-
rily, for my pains, to return instantly to head-quarters.
Keith Armistead, the son of General Armistead who was
killed at Gettysburg, was one of our couriers, and he went
back with me. That night an ineffectual effort was made
by our surgeons to find the ball, which was supposed to be
near the shoulder. General Lee insisted that I should go
back to Petersburg or Richmond, as I preferred. Soon
after daybreak I was told that the enemy had broken our
lines at Petersburg, and I could not return to that place; so
I went to Richmond, where I arrived on Sunday night,
April 2.

Major Warwick had begged that I would go to the house
of his father, Major Abram Warwick, and I had the satisfaction of letting him know that his son was safe. Under the
influence of morphine I went to sleep, notwithstanding the
pain of my wound; and when I awoke in the morning Richmond had been evacuated by the Confederates, and the
enemy were in possession of the city. The Warwicks had
known when I arrived that our troops were about to leave
Richmond, but had refrained from telling me, as they deem-
ed it unsafe to have me moved in the condition in which I
was. It was a sad, sad time. Mrs. W. B. Warwick walked
up and down the long halls almost demented with grief;
and there were other troubles besides those that grew out
of the hazardous condition of the soldiers who had retreated
with Lee. Two days before, Mr. Abram Warwick was one

of the wealthiest men in Richmond, and had almost unlimited means at his command. This Monday morning the great Gallego Mills, of which he was the principal owner, lay in ashes, and he himself was without a dollar of money that would pass current in the city. So it was on every side. Hundreds of families were reduced to absolute beggary by the fire which swept over Richmond. I cannot bear to dwell upon the harrowing scenes of those days. The surgeons made another effort to extract the ball from my shoulder, and came to the wise conclusion that less harm probably would be done by letting it alone than by cutting and carving me in the effort to get it out. So they let me alone, and that ball has never troubled me since.

A week after I reached Richmond I felt strong enough to join the army again, although, of course, I could not use my arm; and Miss Agnes Lee, one of General R. E. Lee's daughters, had arranged that I should be smuggled out of the city, under a bale of hay, in one of the market carts that came into the city with vegetables every morning. Then came the harrowing tidings that General Lee had surrendered. It seemed to us impossible that the Army of Northern Virginia should be no more, and we scouted the first reports that reached us. All too soon, however, General Lee came back to Richmond, and there was no longer room for doubt. The first returning officer whom I knew well was Colonel Manning, who, with the big tears rolling down his cheeks, as he sat gaunt and weary on his horse in Franklin Street, told me the pitiful story of the last days of the army and the circumstances of the surrender. The only consolation to me was that General Fitz Lee and my dear comrades had escaped unhurt, except Minnigerode, who was wounded and in the hands of the enemy, as mentioned previously.

19

There was nothing in the behaviour of the Federal troops to mitigate the unpleasantness of our situation. They did not rob, and they did not kill; but they sought opportunities to humiliate and annoy the defeated Confederates. One of their first orders was that no person should wear clothing with military buttons; and those who had no other buttons but military buttons must cover them so as to conceal their character. After this, the buttons on most of our uniforms, which were the only clothing we had, were covered with crape.

I had lost my desk containing my commissions and papers, which I had left in our head-quarters wagon; but Armistead had put my trunk in the ambulance, and I saved that. Armistead went back to the command as soon as he had placed me in Mr. Warwick's care; and, as he was but poorly armed, I gave him my revolver, which thus was saved from falling into the hands of the enemy. My sabre, which was taken from me on the night that I was wounded, was unfortunately left at head-quarters, and was lost.

The war being virtually at an end, and there being no other way to get out of Richmond, I presented myself to the Provost Marshal and was duly paroled. Then I went over to Petersburg, my whole worldly possessions being a postage stamp and what was left of a five dollar greenback that a friend in Baltimore had sent me. The first thing I did with this greenback, by the way, was to get small change for it so as to make it look big; and the first luxuries that I bought were cigars and oranges.

XXIII.

I went to Petersburg on April 23d. At Petersburg I was invited to make a visit to Mr. William Cameron, and was very glad to accept. All his servants had left him, and Colonel Frank Huger, of the artillery, and I amused ourselves by preparing the table for breakfast and dinner, and were Mrs. Cameron's·chief assistants in cutting vegetables in the garden and in washing up the dishes. I must say that this last process was anything but advantageous, as we contrived between us to break a good deal of our friend's pretty china and delicate glass. The unfortunate things had a horrible way of losing their handles and of coming to pieces, as we scrubbed them with more zeal than discretion.

Early in June, I went to Mechlenburg to see Mr. Raines, who was still living on the plantation which he had rented near the plantation of Dr. Jones; and it was then that I heard of the barbarous conduct of the Federal cavalry on their raid through that neighborhood, and which I have mentioned previously. This raid it will be remembered was made after the surrender of General Lee's army, and when there was no shadow of military justification or excuse for it. Little was wanting to make the conduct of the soldiers utterly execrable, and Dr. Jones escaped better than most of his neighbors. By this time the health of Mrs. Jones was exceedingly feeble, and in the September following she died. Meanwhile, the seeds of consumption were developed in her younger sister, Miss Martha Raines, and she too died a few months afterwards. Consumption also carried off the only remaining sister, Miss Anna Raines, who died, I think, in 1866.

It was rather difficult for me to get back from Mechlenburg to Petersburg, a distance of about one hundred miles; but I borrowed an old horse, and, out of the remains of several old buggies and carriages that were on the place, succeeded in making up what appeared to be a rather respectable vehicle. It did hang together pretty well until I had occasion to cross a river on my route, when the action of the water caused one of the wheels to fall to pieces in the middle of the stream. With considerable difficulty, I dragged what remained of the buggy out of the river, and was fortunate enough to be able to borrow another wheel from a planter near by. The wheel that I borrowed I was to return to him when I should go back to Mechlenburg. As I never went back, the wheel, I grieve to say, was not returned; and, as I do not know the name of my kind friend, it would be vain to try to compensate him for the loss he sustained. What weighs, I think, rather more heavily than this on my conscience, is a commission entrusted to me by an old farmer, on the road, with whom I took supper one night. Finding that I expected to come back in a few days, he asked me if I would bring him a Richmond newspaper, and gave me a silver dime to pay for it. That dime he had saved during the war, and only parted with it from a desire to get some news of what was going on. No doubt he, and the friend who lent me the buggy wheel, think of me to-day as one of the gay deceivers who were abundant after the cessation of hostilities.

While still a good many miles from Petersburg, what with insufficient food and hard driving my horse broke down completely, and I dragged along the rest of the way at the rate of a mile or two an hour. Near Petersburg I stopped to dine with a planter, who, finding that I was an

Englishman, asked me how far it was from London to Windsor. I told him, and he replied that the distance could not be so great, for he remembered an anecdote of the singular experience of one of the sentries at Windsor Castle, who was accused of sleeping on his post. Denying this emphatically, the sentry told the officers that he had heard the bell of St. Paul's, at London, strike at midnight. This was thought to be impossible; but he told them that he not only heard it, but that the bell struck thirteen instead of twelve. It was afterward ascertained that, through some derangement of the machinery of the clock, thirteen had been struck instead of twelve, and the vigilance of the sentry was established. I do not know what the origin of the anecdote was, but it was curious to meet with it in the bosom of Virginia. And this reminds me of the quaint knowledge of things in London that I found here and there in the South. Mr. L. M. Blackford, who was attached to the Military Court of Longstreet's Corps, asked me one day as we were riding along the road, what streets I would take if I wanted to go from one part of London, which he named, to another part. I told him, and he said he thought it would be nearer to take other streets than those I had mentioned. I asked him if he had been to London. He said that he had not, but explained that his father and himself were so much attached to England, and to everything English, that they had studied the map of London, and were almost as familiar with the place, by the map, as if they had lived there. Mr. Blackford, by the way, is now the Principal of the Episcopal High School at Alexandria, Va. I have not seen him since the war, but know that he has been to Europe, and has, therefore, had an opportunity of putting his knowledge of London streets to good account.

My efforts to obtain employment in Petersburg were entirely unsuccessful, although I was not particular about the kind of work. I was on the point of getting an engagement as the driver of a dray, but a stalwart negro, at the last moment, was taken in my place. It was a sensible thing on the part of the employer of the negro, no doubt, but it was mortifying to me that a negro should be allowed to earn his bread, and a white man, who was willing to do the same work, be denied the opportunity.

In July I went over to Richmond, and with a Mr. Evans, (a relative of Mr. Tyler) began arrangements for publishing a small weekly newspaper. My work was to be local reporting and canvassing for advertisements. The type, I think, was borrowed from the Richmond *Whig*, and we got to the point of making up one form, consisting of the first and fourth pages of the forthcoming paper. But the *Whig* had done something to offend the military autocrat who was in command at Richmond, and one fine morning he sent a party of soldiers to the *Whig* office, who took possession of the whole establishment, and closed it up. Our newspaper in embryo was embargoed with the rest of the establishment, and there my first connection with American journalism came to an untimely end.

Returning to Petersburg, I walked down to Mr. Raines' plantation, and there earned something for myself, for the first time since the war had ended. Mr. Raines had returned home, and had cut his wheat crop, which was a very fine one, and, as much to amuse us as any thing else, he told his son Frank and me that, if we would take the horse-rake and glean the fields, we might have what wheat we could find. It was desperately hot work, but we succeeded in getting a considerable quantity of wheat, which Mr. Raines threshed out and sold for us in Petersburg. My share of the proceeds was about $10.

I spoke just now of walking down to the plantation. The distance from Petersburg was about eighteen miles, and I frequently walked it by the middle of the day, leaving Petersburg early in the morning.

One of the Ordnance Sergeants of Longstreet's Corps, John J. Campbell, lived at Petersburg, and I stayed there with him for some time, after my visit to Mr. Cameron. Mrs. Campbell was a plain, unaffected and thoroughly good-hearted woman, and was unremitting in her kindness. Unfortunately there came to be more talking than I liked about my own affairs, and a coolness grew up which I greatly regretted. I mention Mrs. Campbell here, in order to have the satisfaction of showing that, whatever was the cause of the discontinuance of our friendly relations, I am, and always have been, most grateful for her kindness.

Mrs. Andrew White had been zealous in her efforts to secure for me some employment, and to her I was indebted for the clothes which took the place of my Confederate uniform. Through her instrumentality, in October I was engaged by Seldner & Rosenberg, of Petersburg, as book-keeper. I fear that I knew nothing, or next to nothing, about book-keeping. But my employers were not aware of that awkward fact, and I do not think that they discovered it. The pay was $40 a month, and I paid $30 a month for my board. I went to work at half-past six o'clock in the morning, and remained at work until eight o'clock at night. There was not much margin for my personal expenses, and the long hours made the occupation terribly irksome to me, but I had the promise of an advance of pay, and, with that before me, struggled on until November.

In Petersburg one day I saw a Federal officer riding my black horse, which I had sent to Mr. Raines' to recruit during the previous winter, and which had been captured in the raid there after the cessation of hostilities. I claimed the horse at once, and the first difficulty I encountered was the fact that I was not regarded as a citizen of the United States. The officer in command at Petersburg told me that my claim would not be considered, unless I could show that I was an American citizen, or intended to become one. As a matter of fact, I had become a citizen of Virginia, by my service in the Confederate Army. But this was not sufficient for the captors of my charger, so I made no difficulty in fully renouncing before the proper officer at Petersburg my allegiance to every foreign King, Prince or potentate, and more particularly Her Majesty, Queen Victoria. This was my formal "declaration of intention" to become a citizen of the United States, and I received my naturalization papers from Judge Bryan, of the United States District Court, at Charleston, in 1867.

In spite of the greatest economy, I found that my expenses were greater than my income, and I determined to abandon book-keeping in the clothing and dry goods establishment of Seldner & Rosenberg, and try my hand at planting, with Dr. Jones. The understanding with him was that I should assist in managing the plantation under his direction, and receive a portion of the net profit, whatever that might be.

XXXIV.

I closed up my affairs in Petersburg just as the week was drawing to an end, and decided to go to Mechlenburg on Monday morning; but I could not make up my mind to go off without running over to Richmond to bid the Tylers and other friends there good-bye. When I went into Mr. Tyler's house, where, as ever, my reception was most hearty, Dr. C. W. Brock, Mr. Tyler's son-in-law, asked me whether I had received a telegram he had sent me. I told him that I had not, and he then informed me, to my astonishment, that Mr. H. Rives Pollard, who had been one of the editors of the *Examiner* during the war, was about to resume the publication of that paper, and wanted me to take a place on the staff, as local reporter. I was in much the same mood that I was in when I received my commission as Ordnance Officer, in 1862, and told Brock that I knew nothing about local reporting. But he insisted that it was too good an opportunity to lose, and that I must close with Pollard at once, and trust to work and luck for the rest. Pollard was quite cordial, and told me that he would give me $20 a week. This change from $40 a month to $80 a month gave me a feeling of wealth that I am sure I have never had since. It seemed to me that there were no bounds to the results that might be accomplished with so vast a sum. Pollard had issued a flaming prospectus, in which he described the different members of the staff. As I was unknown to journalistic fame I did not appear on the roll. One of the conspicuous figures, however, was Mr. B. R. Riordan, who, in the words of the prospectus, was an " experienced and accomplished young journalist, who had

20

been for a number of years one of the editors of the New Orleans *Delta*, and who, during the war, had been the managing editor of the Charleston *Mercury*." Those were the words, or very nearly so, and I was profoundly impressed, I remember, with the journalistic grandeur of the forthcoming journalist from the South. Pollard was busily engaged in his room, and had refused to see any one, when a rather slender and exceedingly quiet looking man came in, and told me that he wanted to see Mr. Pollard. I told him that Pollard was engaged, and could not be disturbed, whereupon he told me, very composedly, that he expected that Mr. Pollard would see him, and, without more ado, passed by me and walked into Pollard's room. This was my first introduction to Mr. B. R. Riordan.

Pollard was a queer character; not without ability, but lazy, vain and dissolute, and it was not very easy, therefore, to make the *Examiner* what he wanted it to be. Under the editorial management of Mr. John Daniel during the war, the *Examiner* was known everywhere for its great ability and its caustic criticisms of the conduct of the war by Mr. Davis and his Cabinet. It was a brilliant newspaper, but disfigured by the whim of Mr. Daniel that the old English form of spelling words ending in "c" should be retained, so that in the *Examiner* such words as "antic," "critic," and "music," were spelled with a final k. Pollard insisted upon retaining this peculiarity. But this did not make up for the loss of the brain and vigor of Mr. Daniel. Professor Gildersleeve, of the University of Virginia, and other erudite men, were engaged as editorial writers, but they did not live in Richmond, and their work was often stale. Pollard hacked and cooked their articles to suit himself, and, when the supply of new material failed, had

no hesitation in revamping and republishing articles which
had appeared in the *Examiner* during the war. However,
I had no reason to complain of Pollard's treatment of me.
Amongst other things, he was always exceedingly anxious
to resent any affront that might be put upon him, and this
weakness, if such it should be called, enabled me to make
myself indispensable. I occupied the unpleasant position, as
I should now consider it, of adviser and best man for Pollard
in his principal rencontres.

The first of these grew out of an article in the Richmond
Enquirer which reflected on the *Examiner*, and caused
Pollard to determine to cowhide the editor of the *Enquirer*
as soon as he could find him. When we ran the *Enquirer*
man to earth, he was in the hall of the House of Repre-
sentatives at the Capitol, and Pollard waited for him in
the rotunda. When the *Enquirer* man came out, Pollard
attempted to strike him and was resisted. Both the
Enquirer man and Pollard drew pistols, and several shots
were exchanged. Only one shot, however, took effect, and
it unfortunately carried away the tassel of the cane on
Houdon's statue of George Washington, which is in the
centre of the rotunda. The combatants were arrested, and
for a few days there was peace.

The next offender was E. P. Brooks, of the New York
Times. In a letter from Richmond he spoke rather abusively
of Pollard, and Pollard decided to give him a beating. It
was not very easy to find him at first, as neither Pollard
nor I had ever seen him. After a long hunt I was told that
he was in the billiard room at the Spotswood Hotel, and I
succeeded in getting a good look at him. Pollard. came
down immediately, armed to the teeth and flourishing a big
cowhide, and, when Brooks came into the lobby of the hotel,

accosted him and asked whether he was the Richmond correspondent of the New York *Times*. Brooks told him that
he was, and thereupon Pollard seized him by the collar and
began to thrash him soundly. Several persons attempted
to interfere, but I kept them off with my pistol until the
affair was at an end. Brooks had pulled a handful of hair
out of Pollard's long beard, and Pollard had jammed Brooks'
head through the glass partition in front of the desk, and
had given him some hard blows besides. Pollard was not
in good society in Richmond, but the Brooks affair was
much enjoyed. When I told a drawing-room full of ladies
about it, they clapped their hands with joy that the "miserable Yankee" should have been so well thrashed by the
Southerner.

The next cloud of war was on account of Mrs. Henningsen, wife of General Henningsen, whom the *Examiner* had
spoken of as a "notorious" character. This was not to be
a street fight, but a regular duel according to the "Code."
Pollard placed himself in my hands, and I had a mischievous
pleasure in telling him that General Henningsen, who had
demanded an apology for the insult offered his wife, was a
crack shot, and could hit the spots on a card at fifteen paces
with a duelling pistol, nine times out of ten. Pollard told
me, in some little trepidation, that he did not believe he could
hit a barn door at ten paces, and I warned him that it was
high time that he was practicing. Pollard evidently did not
hanker after a fight this time, and I succeeded in arranging
the matter amicably.

A little later somebody else trod on Pollard's toes, and
he determined to "post" him. Preceded by a negro boy
bearing a paste pot and brush and a number of hand bills
or posters, denouncing the person to be posted as a liar,

coward, and a variety of other things, Pollard marched down Main Street with a double-barrelled shotgun on his shoulder and a huge revolver and bowie knife in a belt around his waist. There was no fight, and I am not sure that the man who was posted was in Richmond.

I have said that Pollard was a man of loose character, and he was very careless in the statements he made affecting any one's reputation if he could, by the publication, make a hit for his paper. Yet, strange to say, he was killed for an offence which he did not commit himself, although he was responsible for it. In 1867, the paper he was managing (the *Examiner* having died previously) published a flaming account of the elopement of a Miss Grant, of Richmond. It was written up very elaborately, and highly spiced. It was expected that trouble would come of it, but it was not supposed that Pollard would be denied the chance to defend himself. James Grant, the brother of the lady who was the subject of the article in the *Examiner*, ensconced himself in a room in a house which Pollard passed regularly every morning. It was near his office. As Pollard passed by the window of the room, Grant, who was hidden from sight, shot Pollard down with a double-barrelled gun. He died instantly, and without knowing who killed him. Grant was tried for murder, and was acquitted. The feeling in Richmond was very strong against Grant; not because he had killed Pollard, but because he had not confronted him like a man, and given him a chance for his life. All this was long after I left Richmond.

Mr. Riordan and I were now on very good terms. We slept in one of the rooms at the *Examiner* office, in which we worked, and took our meals together at Zetelle's restaurant. I suppose I must have made a good impression upon him, as I find the following in a letter to my mother, dated January 11, 1866: "Our news editor, a gentleman of ten or fifteen years experience in the newspaper business, says that it is impossible that a man of my talent can remain unemployed, and Pollard says he is delighted with my fluency, style and indefatigable energy. Of course, I do not place one particle of reliance in such remarks as these. They are sincere, and I am grateful for them, but these gentlemen cannot make me think so highly of myself as they seem to think of me." About this time Mr. Riordan, the news editor just mentioned, broached to me a plan for starting a cheap and popular newspaper in Charleston, South Carolina. He said that the Charleston newspapers were very slow and old fashioned, and that there was a fine field for a new and bright paper. This he had thought for a long time, but had not taken any steps to give the project shape, because he had not found the right sort of man to go into it with him. He was pleased to say that I was just the man he was looking for, and that he was quite sure that he and I could make the paper successful. The whole of the details of the prospective newspaper were carefully discussed. It is rather amusing to recall now Riordan's remark that the local reporting in Charleston need not give us much trouble, as the policemen would drop in and tell us about anything that happened. Another remark of his was about in these words: "Of course you know Dawson you could not do the editorial writing, but we could engage a man to do that for us." Riordan, like myself, had no money, but thought that he had friends who would lend us some; and this was the position of affairs when my connection with the *Examiner* was suddenly suspended.

XXXV.

The Federal officers in Richmond gave several public dancing parties, or "Hops" as they were called, at the different hotels, and desired that the Richmond ladies should attend them. There was, of course, too much feeling against the North at this time to permit anything of the sort, and the only Richmond women who attended these "Hops" were the wives and daughters of the present and prospective office holders under the United States Government. The newspapers were not invited to send reporters to the "Hops," but the *Examiner* managed always to have a man there, and gave a highly colored report of them the morning after the occurrence, describing and naming the Richmond people who were there, and dressing up the whole account in a style of mingled bitterness and ridicule. J. Marshall Hanna, the principal local reporter for the *Examiner*, did most of the work on these reports, and it was he, by the way, who described the elopement of Miss Grant which had so tragical consequences. The Federal officers were indignant at the way in which their efforts at reconciliation were treated by the *Examiner*, but another "Hop" was announced. This was in March, 1866. We prepared ourselves for a report that should out-Herod Herod. Hanna, Mr. Fred. Daniel, and I were engaged on it, and we called into requisition every apt quotation we could find in French and Italian, as well as in English. The report being finished, I went to a ball to which I had been invited, and did not return to the office until near daylight. At the office door I found a sentry, who halted me and refused to allow me to pass into the building. To my astonishment I then learned that the

Federal Commandant at Richmond had taken possession of the *Examiner* office, and had suspended its publication, on account of the malignant and disloyal reports of the famous Yankee " Hops." It was with great difficulty that I induced the guard to allow me to go up to my room for more suitable attire. Riordan told me that he was at his desk working quietly on his exchanges, when he heard a dull tramp, tramp in the street, and then tramp, tramp on the stairs, and then tramp, tramp in the outer room, and the command " halt!" and the rattle of muskets on the floor. By this time he began to think that something unusual was happening, and was sure of it when an officer entered the room and told him that he had orders to seize the whole establishment, and that he and everyone else connected with the paper must leave the place at once. This arbitrary and lawless proceeding did not shock me as much as it ought to have done, inasmuch as it held out the promise of a holiday, which I knew I could pass delightfully with my fair friends in Richmond ; but the very day that the *Examiner* was shut up the proprietors of the Richmond *Dispatch* sent for me, and offered me a salary of $25 a week if I would go on the staff of that paper. Mr. Pollard made no objection, and I went to work at once on the *Dispatch*. The *Examiner* remained in possession of the military authorities for about two weeks I think, and was only released when a peremptory order to that end was given by the President himself.

On the *Dispatch* I was legislative and local reporter, and was handsomely treated. One of my colleagues was Captain J. Innes Randolph, who had played that 'possum trick on me at Bunker Hill, on the retreat from Gettysburg. Randolph was a man of many accomplishments. He played the piano and violin charmingly, was a skillful engineer, a very capable lawyer, and wrote charmingly in both prose and verse. "The Good Old Rebel" is one of his productions, and his lines on the statue of Marshall, which now stands in the Capitol Square, are worth remembering. Randolph is the son of Lieutenant Randolph of the Navy, who tweaked President Jackson's nose, and has something of his father's temper. A more cranky and irritable fellow is rarely met with. He lives in Baltimore, and is now on the staff of the *American*. I have not seen him for several years.

21

XXXVI

It was in the spring of 1866 that I was instrumental in forming what I believe to have been the first of the Confederate Memorial Associations in the Southern States. This is the Hollywood Memorial Association, of Richmond. In Hollywood Cemetery are interred fifteen thousand or sixteen thousand Confederate soldiers, and in Oakwood Cemetery are as many more. Their graves were entirely uncared for, and I began in the *Dispatch* to agitate the subject, with a view to forming an association which should undertake to keep the graves in order, mark them suitably, and erect a monument to our dead. The earliest fruit of it was a suspension of business on the first Memorial day, when hundreds of young men who had belonged to different military organizations went out to Hollywood, accompanied by ladies bearing flowers, and labored for several hours with spade and hoe in rearranging the mounds over the graves, and clearing away the rank growth of weeds. The ladies of the Hollywood Association were most enthusiastic, and I acted as their Secretary. Public meetings were held in the Churches in furtherance of the objects of the Association, and in June I addressed three meetings of ladies on one day, at different places. One of these meetings was at the Monumental Church, and about five hundred ladies were present. There were two different plans. One was to level the graves and erect a general monument; and the other was to mark each one of the graves with a headstone bearing either the name of the soldier who lay there, or a number by which, on reference to the books of the Cemetery, the name of the soldier could be known. I pleaded for the

plan that would keep each grave separate and distinct, and
would allow any father or mother, or sister or brother, from
the far South to know the identical spot where the bones
of their dear one lay, rather than that they should be shown
a vast open area and be told that somewhere within those
bounds their young hero lay buried. I was modest in those
days, and, when one of the ladies at the close of the meeting
told me that she wanted to kiss me for my speech, I blushed
and declined. As long as I was in Richmond I continued
to work actively for the Memorial Association, and, when I
left Richmond to come to Charleston, I received from the
President a letter, of which the following is a copy:

RICHMOND, November 8, 1866.

My Dear Sir—As the organ of the Hollywood Memorial Association, I desire to express to you our grateful acknowledgment of your untiring efforts in
our behalf, and our sense of your valuable and disinterested services in advancing our solemn and sacred purpose.

Your taste and ardor have been efficient in securing for us a large share of
general sympathy.

We sincerely regret to lose you from our counsels, but feel assured of your
continued sympathy and interest, as you may of our best wishes for your success
and happiness.

Be pleased to accept our acknowledgments, and with them the accompanying slight memorial.

I am, with high respect, your friend,

N. MACFARLAND,
President H. M. A.

To Captain F. W. DAWSON.

The "slight memorial" of which Mrs. Macfarland speaks
is a set of studs and sleeve buttons of gold, with the Confederate battle-flag in enamel on each one. I hope that my
children will prize these; not only because they bear upon
them the flag under which their father fought, but because
of the source whence they came, and the work and sympathy they commemorate.

I had much to do with another undertaking of a totally

different character. My immediate circle of friends, among the men in Richmond, consisted of Captain Philip H. Haxall, who had been on General Lee's staff for a short time; Charlie Minnigerode, whom I have spoken of before, and who was now fast recovering from his wound; Willie Myers, who married a niece of Captain Pegram, Miss Mattie Paul, and died of consumption, dear fellow, some years ago; Page McCarty, who afterwards blighted his life by killing Mordecai in a duel; Jack Elder, the artist; and John Dunlop, my old Petersburg friend, and a few others. We had been in the habit of meeting at night, when we had any time to spare, in what we called "the chicken coop," which was a sort of summer-house in the rear of a restaurant in Broad Street. Here we founded the Richmond Club, of which Colonel D. G. MacIntosh, of South Carolina, who had married the beautiful Virginia Pegram, and was then living in Richmond, was the first President. I was the first Secretary. I mention the Richmond Club here, because it soon grew to be a large and prosperous concern, with a handsome club house of its own, and because there were features in the constitution and by-laws which might be adopted with advantage by similar associations. Card-playing for money was absolutely prohibited, and what was more peculiar than this, and was a hobby of my own, no member was allowed to take any refreshments whatever in the club at the expense of another. No "treating" was permitted, unless a stranger should have been invited to the club by a member, in which case the member who invited him might ask other friends to join the party. It was an admirable rule, and was effectual in preventing that hard drinking which is the bane of most clubs, and which is difficult, at times, to avoid so long as one member feels under any obligation, or is permitted, to invite other members to drink with him at his expense, which involves an obligation on their part to return the compliment.

My health now was not as good as it had been. I was attacked by chills and fever, and obliged to give up my work. I think the malady was brought on by my exposure to the sun, in my tramps about the streets in the summer. Dr. Barney, of Richmond, insisted upon my going to his house, and Mrs. Barney was assiduous in her kindness. As soon as I began to regain my strength I went up to Mr. Barton Haxall's beautiful place, near Orange Courthouse, and recovered rapidly. This was in August or September, 1866. I had for a short time been engaged to be married to Miss Mary Haxall, one of Mr. Haxall's daughters, but was unceremoniously jilted not long before I went up to Orange. A brighter or wittier girl than Mary Haxall, in those days, it were hard to find; and the unkindest cut of all was that she should have ended by marrying a man whom she might never have known had I not presented him to her. This is Mr. Alexander Cameron, a wealthy tobacco manufacturer of Richmond, who is, I am told, desperately in love with his wife after all these years, and proves his affection by allowing her to have her own way in everything. Before my engagement to her, I was at a party as her escort, when Mr. George, of Richmond, appeared discourteous in his conduct towards her, in consequence of a difference of opinion as to an engagement to dance. As soon as I had conducted her home I sent Mr. George a challenge. Page McCarty acted as my friend, in the matter; and part of his plan of action was to have the ground for the combat on the other side of Hollywood Cemetery, so that the duelists would have the satisfaction of passing through or around the Cemetery on their way to the place of meeting. Page told me, with his peculiar drawl, that he knew I could stand it, and he thought it might unsettle the nerves of the other fellow. The whole of the arrangements had been made, and we were to fight the next morning, when some cool headed friend (I do not remember who it was), intervened, and the difficulty was adjusted, as it ought to have been. There was so little expectation of a settlement that I made a visit to Miss Jennie Cooper, the daughter of Adjutant-General Cooper, late in the evening, and communicated to her my last wishes; and gave her my watch to take care of, and dispose of, in the event that the walk through the Cemetery should not have the expected effect upon Mr. George's nerves. My experience with Miss Haxall prompts me to say that an attractive girl is exceedingly dangerous to the peace of mind of any one whom she may undertake to instruct in the round dances. The crisis was brought on, I believe, by some tableaux for the benefit of the Memorial Association, or something of that kind. In the tableaux Miss Mary was "Cleopatra" and I was a Confederate soldier lying dead on the battle-field, wearing for the occasion the uniform coat of Major McGraw, who was a Lieutenant in the Purcell Battery in 1862, when I joined it, and had risen to the rank of Major and lost an arm in the service. It was the morning after the tableaux that I became engaged to Miss Mary, and presented her with a gold brooch which exhausted my pocket money, and on which brooch her initials and mine were tenderly scratched with the point of a pin. In less than a fortnight the play was over. But when I returned to Richmond, from Orange, I went to see Miss Mary and her sister Miss Lottie Haxall, who were then making a visit to

Mr. Conway Robinson, their uncle. who lives near the Soldier's Home at Washington. Miss Lottie Haxall, the younger sister of Miss Mary, was a thoroughly high-bred girl in every way, and noble in every phase of her character.

XXXVII.

I had pretty well made up my mind to leave the *Dispatch* if I should receive an offer of employment elsewhere. There was no prospect of advancement in the *Dispatch* office, and I was very much disgusted by the intention of the proprietors to stop my pay during my absence on account of my illness, contracted in their service. When I returned to Richmond I was sent for by Colonel Briscoe G. Baldwin, who had been Chief Ordnance officer of General Lee's army, and had been appointed Superintendent of the National Express Company. He told me he wanted me to take a position under him in the National Express Company. This company was organized after the war as a rival of the Southern Express Company, and had been something of a hospital for Confederate officers of high rank. It was at this time in a tottering condition; but Colonel Baldwin said he thought it was not too late to save it, if he could get such men as he wanted to do the active work of the Company. He did not pretend to hide the condition of the Company from me, but told me that he desired to have me there and thought that it would be a good place for me, as, if the Company did pull through its difficulties, I would be on the sure road to promotion. I resigned from the *Dispatch*, and on September 17th, 1866, I was appointed Route Agent in the National Express and Transportation Company, "with all the rights, privileges, authority, and duties attaching to the position." My salary was one hundred dollars a month, and the Company paid my travelling expenses. The territory which I was to supervise covered the lines of railroad from Richmond to Alexandria in one direction, and from Richmond to Bristol, Tennessee, in the other. I went out on the road at once, visiting the agents at every depot, and examining into the condition of the business. There was great confusion everywhere, and the railroads were threatening to discontinue taking freight for us, as the Company did not pay the charges promptly. One of the places that I visited was Lexington, where I had the great happiness of seeing General R. E. Lee and his daughters again. I saw General Lee only once after this, and that was when he visited Charleston not long before he died. Engaged as he was with visitors, he gave me, in kindly remembrance of my services with his nephew, General Fitzhugh Lee, a private interview, in order that my wife, Virginia, might be presented to him. General Lee's youngest son, Robert E. Lee, married Miss Lottie Haxall. I heard after I left Richmond that they would probably become engaged, but I lost sight of Miss Lottie until 1872, when I heard that Mr. and Mrs. R. E. Lee, who were newly married, were staying at Aiken. Assuming that Mrs. Lee must be my old friend Miss Lottie, I wrote to her and begged her to come to Charleston. A night or two afterwards I was at the theatre in Charleston, and as I looked at the audience I saw her sparkling face turned towards me and smiling recognition. The next day Mr. and Mrs. Lee spent with me and my wife, and we went down to Fort Sumter together. It was the last time that my wife went out; and only two or three months afterwards Lottie Lee died of consumption. Almost the last words that my wife, Virginia, who died in 1872, said to me before her death were: "When I die, I shall see Lottie again."

I also had the opportunity of visiting Warrenton, where I spent a day with General W. H. Payne, whom I had not

22

seen since we bade each other goodbye when he was wounded at Five Forks. General Lomax was living near Warrenton, and we had a glorious day reviving the memories of our service in the cavalry. The National Express Company, however, was on its last legs; and when I reached Richmond in October I found that it had been determined to wind up the concern. So ended my career as an expressman. While on one of my tours of inspection, and waiting at a wayside station for the train, I wrote the following verses:

"ONLY A PRIVATE."

I.

Only a private! his jacket of gray
    Is stained by the smoke and the dust;
As Bayard, he's brave; as Rupert, he's gay;
Reckless as Murat in heat of the fray,
    But in God is his only trust!

II.

Only a private! to march and to fight,
    To suffer and starve and be strong;
With knowledge enough to know that the might
Of justice, and truth, and freedom and right,
    In the end must crush out the wrong.

III.

Only a private! no ribbon or star
    Shall gild with false glory his name!
No honors for him in braid or in bar,
His Legion of Honor is only a scar,
    And his wounds are his roll of fame!

IV.

Only a private! one more hero slain
    On the field lies silent and chill!
And in the far South a wife prays in vain
One clasp of the hand she may ne'er clasp again,
    One kiss from the lips that are still.

V.

Only a private ! there let him sleep !
    He will need nor tablet nor stone ;
For the mosses and vines o'er his grave will creep,
And at night the stars through the clouds will peep,
    And watch him who lies there alone.

VI.

Only a martyr ! who fought and who fell
    Unknown and unmarked in the strife !
But still as he lies in his lonely cell
Angel and Seraph the legend shall tell—
    Such a death is eternal life !

Richmond, Va., October 24, 1866.

XXXVIII.

Riordan did not remain long with the *Examiner* after I left it, and had been at work in Washington. Occasionally he wrote to me, and assured me that he had not given up the newspaper project for Charleston, and that he would put a "peg in" in that direction whenever he had an opportunity. With this in view, he accepted a position offered him on the Charleston *Courier*, and went back to Charleston. In October, Colonel R. Barnwell Rhett was preparing to resume the publication of the *Mercury*, and asked Riordan to take his old place on that paper. Riordan declined to do this, and advised Colonel Rhett to take me if I would come. It was only a day, or two after I had finished my work with the National Express Company that I received a letter from Riordan, telling me what he had done; and on the heels of his letter came a telegram from Colonel Rhett, offering me an engagement on the *Mercury* and asking me to come to Charleston immediately. There was nothing to require me to remain in Richmond, so I accepted Colonel Rhett's offer, and after a round of leave-taking started for Charleston, where I arrived on November 10th, 1866.

My first visit was to Riordan, whom I found in the *Courier* office in East Bay Street. The next day I went to work in the *Mercury* office, and remained on that paper until Riordan and I bought one-third of the Charleston *News* in the autum of 1867. On May 1, 1867, I was married to Miss Virginia Fourgeaud, a faithful and loving wife. Her health unhappily failed fast, and she died in December, 1872.

In the waning fortunes of the Charleston *News* was the opportunity that we had long desired of becoming mana-

gers of a newspaper of our own; an object which Riordan
had kept unflaggingly in view from the moment that he had
first talked the project over with me in the *Examiner* office
at Richmond.   It was his foresight, of course, in seizing the
opportunity to bring me to Charleston, that put us both in
the position to take the chance which was presented to us
by the decline of the Charleston *News*.   The paper had
been exceedingly successful under extravagant and careless
management, and we could not, of course, expect to obtain
control of it until those who were managing it in Charleston were willing to give it up.   Captain James F. McMillan
and Mr. R. S. Cathcart had been controlling the paper.   Cathcart withdrew, and the condition of the paper grew worse.
It was heavily in debt, and the proprietors of the *Courier*
and *Mercury* looked cheerfully forward to the time when it
should quietly expire.   We found that the real owner of
the property was Mr. Benjamin Wood, of New York, and
Riordan went on to New York to open negotiations with
him.   This ended in Mr. Wood buying out Mr. McMillan,
and in our purchasing one-third of the property at the rate
of $18,000 for the whole.   The new concern, of which
Benjamin Wood was a member, as the representative of
Henry Evans, a person in his employment, assumed all
the liabilities of the old concern.   Riordan and I, therefore,
found ourselves owners of one-third of a newspaper which had
a *bona fide* circulation of twenty-five hundred, or three thous-
and, copies daily, with debts amounting to nearly $20,000,
and property consisting of two very old presses, a broken
down engine, and a suit of badly worn type.   But we
were very cheerful about it, and our confident expectation
was that, in about five years, we should be able to retire
from newspaper work, in part, and live at our ease on the

property we had accumulated. It did not turn out exactly in that way; but, as all the subsequent operations of the concern are set forth in general terms in the record of the litigation in which we were involved by Mr. Wood's rascality, it is not necessary to describe them here. I should, however, record the fact, that the money with which I paid for my share of the paper was borrowed from Mr. W. J. Magrath. He advised me strongly against embarking in the venture, but, when I insisted upon doing so, he gave me every assistance in his power.

Some day, perhaps, I may undertake to write the inside history of my connection with the Charleston *News*, and THE NEWS AND .COURIER, and give my experiences in South Carolina politics from 1867 down to the present time. But I cannot do it now; and, indeed, I am too near to the events, and to the persons I should describe, to write as candidly as would be necessary to bring out the whole truth, and make it entirely clear. It would be, I fancy—if I had the time to refresh my memory, by looking over the newspapers for the last fifteen years—a narrative, in its way, quite as interesting, to my friends at least, as the incidents of Confederate service which I have attempted to portray.

XXXIX.

I append to these reminiscences, to complete the record, copies of my parole and of some letters of which I retain the originals.

LETTER FROM THE HOLLYWOOD MEMORIAL ASSOCIATION.

The Ladies of the Hollywood Memorial Association tender to Captain Dawson their heartfelt thanks for his untiring devotion to their cause ; for the efficiency and aid extended to their efforts when most needed ; and the prompt co-operation in all measures adopted by the Association ; and beg leave to say that while they regret his absence from the meeting yesterday afternoon, they recall with pleasure and gratitude the noble work in which he was then engaged.

May the success and energy which crowns that effort be the earnest for the future of the Association, the ladies of which will always hold in grateful remembrance the effective support rendered by Captain Dawson.

Tuesday Morning, May 29th, 1866.

[The work alluded to, I think, was that of preparing for calling out the old soldiers in Richmond to put the graves at Hollywood in order.]

MY PAROLE.

HEAD-QUARTERS DEPARTMENT OF VIRGINIA, ⎰
Richmond, Va., April 18th, 1865. ⎱

I, Captain F. W. Dawson, C. S. A., Prisoner of War, do hereby give my solemn parole of honor not to take part in hostilities against the government of the United States until properly exchanged ; and that I will not do anything directly or indirectly to the disparagement of the authority of the United States until properly exchanged as aforesaid.

(Signed)   FRANCIS W. DAWSON,
Captain and Chief Ordnance Officer Cavalry Corps,
Army of Northern Virginia.

I certify that F. W. Dawson gave the foregoing parole in my presence, and signed it in duplicate.

(Signed)   D. M. EVANS,
Colonel and Provost Marshal.

Richmond, Va., April 18th, 1865.

The bearer, Captain F. W. Dawson, having taken the oath of parole, has permission to go to his home in Mechlenburg County, Va.

LETTER OF COLONEL BALDWIN, CHIEF ORDNANCE OFFICER ARMY NORTHERN VIRGINIA.

RICHMOND, VA., April, 1865.

Captain F. W. DAWSON,

Chief Ordnance Officer Fitz Lee's Cavalry Division :

CAPTAIN—The recent surrender of the Army of Northern Virginia dissolves our official relations for the present. I take pleasure in expressing my high sense of the zeal, intelligence, and courage you have manifested in the discharge of your duties.

Hoping you may soon recover from your wounds, and wishing you a speedy re-union with your friends,

I remain, with much esteem,

Yours, truly,

BRISCOE G. BALDWIN,

Lt.-Col., Chief Ordnance Officer Army Northern Virginia.

LETTER OF COLONEL MANNING, CHIEF ORDNANCE OFFICER 1st CORPS ARMY NORTHERN VIRGINIA.

RICHMOND, VA., April 19th, 1865.

DEAR CAPTAIN—The recent reverses to our armies, and your wound, have for a time relieved you from command. I trust by the time your health is restored that some arrangement may be made to effect your exchange, and allow you to again enter the field, and our country to have the services of an officer who has by his faithfulness, activity, and courage, added no little to the cause which he has adopted ; and won for himself a name which will long be respected and admired where honor and courage are recognized.

Believe me, very truly,

PEYTON L. MANNING,

Lt.-Col., Chief Ordnance Officer 1st Corps
Army of Northern Virginia.

CERTIFICATE OF GENERAL FITZ LEE.

PETERSBURG, April 26th, 1865.

To Captain F. W. DAWSON,

Chief Ordnance Officer Fitz Lee's Cavalry Division :

I hereby certify that Captain Francis W. Dawson, C. S. Ordnance, was regularly commissioned, and at the time of the surrender of the Army of Northern Virginia was on my staff as Chief Ordnance Officer of the Cavalry Corps.

FITZ LEE, *Major-General.*

LETTER OF MR. COWARDIN, SENIOR EDITOR OF THE RICH-MOND DISPATCH.

RICHMOND, September 10th, 1866.

Captain F. W. DAWSON:

My Dear Sir—As you are about to separate your connection with the *Dispatch*, please accept this expression of my sentiments on the occasion.

The *Dispatch* will miss your valuable contributions and your intelligent and persevering efforts to promote its interests, and increase its attractions. I can truly say that I never knew a gentleman more earnest and energetic, in the pursuit of journalism, while you have displayed accomplishments for the profession that are rare and invaluable. Socially, we will all feel a great loss in parting with you ; and the recollections of our intercourse with you will always be agreeable. While your own talents and bearing will command respect for you in every community, and your gallantry in the Southern cause will commend you to the hospitality and friendship of every Southern man, I tender you my most earnest and heartfelt good wishes for your prosperity and happiness in life.

Very truly and sincerely, yours,

J. A. COWARDIN,
Editor Dispatch.

The following is a copy of my application for membership in the Survivors' Association of Charleston District, with the endorsements of the officers under whom I had served :

APPLICATION.

CHARLESTON, S. C., April 14, 1869.

To the Officers and Members of the Survivors' Association of Charleston District, Charleston, S. C. :

GENTLEMEN—The undersigned respectfully applies for admission into your Association, and presents the following as the RECORD of his services in the Confederate Army and Navy :

ENTERED CONFEDERATE SERVICE in December, 1861, at Southampton, England, as sailor, aboard the C. S. Steamer *Nashville*. Promoted to Master's Mate, C. S. N., February, 1862. Resigned as Master's Mate, C. S. N., June, 1862. Entered Purcell Battery, Field's Brigade, Army Northern Virginia, as Private, June, 1862. Promoted to First Lieutenant of Artillery, August, 1862. Promoted to Captain of Artillery, April, 1864.*

---

* Served from June, 1862, to October, 1864, as Assistant Ordnance Officer, 1st Corps, Army of Northern Virginia, and from that time to April, 1865, as Ordnance Officer Fitzhugh Lee's Cavalry Division.

23

PRESENT AT THE FOLLOWING ENGAGEMENTS: Mechanicsville, Second Manassas, Fredericksburg, Gettysburg, Chattanooga, Knoxville, Wilderness, Spottsylvania C. H., North side James River, 1864, Valley of Virginia, 1864, Five Forks.

WOUNDED at Mechanicsville, June 26, 1862; at Harrisonburg, Va., 1864; at Five Forks, March 31, 1865.

TAKEN PRISONER near Williamsport, Va., September 14, 1862. RELEASED on parole, October, 1862.

SURRENDERED and was paroled, May, 1865.

FRANCIS W. DAWSON,
Applicant.

ENDORSEMENTS.

[From Commodore Pegram.]

PETERSBURG, VA., October 29, 1869.

I take pleasure in bearing testimony to the authenticity of the accompanying record, as furnished by Captain F. W. Dawson, whilst he was under my command on board of the C. S. Steamer *Nashville ;* and I do most earnestly recommend him to the favorable consideration of the Committee on Applications, as one eminently entitled, by his efficient services, to enjoy all the advantages and honors of a Survivor.

Captain Dawson offered his services to the Confederate cause on board the C. S. Steamer *Nashville,* at Southampton, England, December, 1861, in any capacity I might designate. He was under age at the time, being about 17 or 18 years old ; for this reason I declined to take him away from his home and friends to set him adrift in a foreign land then engaged in a bloody war.

A few days before sailing from Southampton, duty called me to London, and Dawson, taking advantage of my absence, assumed the garb of a sailor boy, and was enlisted by the First Lieutenant on board the *Nashville.* I did not know that he was on board until we were at sea, and was so surprised at seeing him that I called him to enquire how he had thus gotten the weather-gage of me ? He replied, he was determined to espouse the Confederate cause at all hazards, even by smuggling himself on board, if indispensable to attain his object.

During the voyage of the *Nashville* homeward, the admirable conduct of young Dawson attracted my attention, and that of all the officers ; and such favorable reports were made to me of his zeal in the discharge of every duty required of him, that I determined to give him an acting appointment of Master's Mate in the C. S. Navy, which appointment was promptly confirmed by the Honorable Secretary of the Navy, upon my recommendation, when the *Nashville* arrived at Beaufort, N. C.

Mr. Dawson was attached to a vessel of the James River Squadron at the time that General McClellan made his advance upon Richmond, yet such was his anxiety to engage in the battle, that he offered his services as a volunteer to the officer in command of the Purcell Battery. He was taken from the field of battle at Mechanicsville badly wounded, but remained fighting his gun until the close of the action, when, from loss of blood, he was completely prostrated. Mr. Dawson's bravery on this occasion, elicited the admiration of his Captain, who went with me to the Hon. G. W. Randolph, then Secretary of War, to request that he might be appointed a Lieutenant in the C. S. Army. The request was readily granted as a reward of merit.

Though suffering from a painful wound, Mr. Dawson did not remain idle. An invitation had been issued by the Secretary of War to the junior officers of the army, to propose for admission into the Ordnance Corps. An examination was ordered ; and when the Board of Examiners met, Mr. Dawson was examined and passed with distinction, and was commissioned in the Corps of Ordnance. His career of duty in that branch of the service is better known to the officers of the army with whom he served than to myself: though I have watched his course with great satisfaction, and always felt a profound interest in his advancement and welfare, having long since forgiven him for his tact in weathering an old sailor.

R. B. PEGRAM,

Lt. Com'g, C. S. N.

[*From Lieutenant-General Longstreet.*]

I take pleasure in certifying to the services of Captain Dawson in the 1st Corps, Army of Northern Virginia.

JAMES LONGSTREET,

Lt.-Gen., C. S. A.

[*From Lieutenant-General Anderson.*]

CHARLESTON, S. C., April 16, 1869.

It affords me pleasure to recommend this application to the favorable consideration of the Committee on Applications, and to say that the services rendered by the applicant eminently entitle him to share the privileges and distinctions of a Survivor.

My acquaintance with Captain Dawson began in the early part of the war ; but during a period of about six months, following the battle of the Wilderness, (whilst in command of Longstreet's Corps,) I had constant opportunities to observe the meritorious conduct and gallant bearing of this officer.

The record given within, between the dates or during the period above mentioned, is correct.

R. H. ANDERSON,

Lt.-Gen'l, C. S. A.

[*From Major-General Fitz Lee.*]

RICHLAND, STAFFORD CO., VA., November 10, 1869.

Captain F. W. Dawson was my Ordnance Officer at the time he specifies. He was a brave soldier and an efficient officer.

" Survivors !" let him in.

FITZHUGH LEE,
Maj.-Gen., C. S. A.

These pages I have written at the request of my wife, Sarah Morgan Dawson, and for her dear sake. It is little enough, in the hurry of a busy life, to do for one who, year after year and so long as I have known her, has strengthened my faith by believing in me, and enlarges my hope always by her confidence and love.

APPENDIX:
Wartime Letters to Family and Friends in England
(From originals in the Duke University Library)

My dearest Parents:

This afternoon at 3 o'clock we arrived here, and to my great joy I am now able to send you a letter before reaching the Southern States.

Our trip so far has been most uneventful! On the 3d, Feby orders were suddenly given to fire-up and 2 hours afterwards we were steaming out of Southampton Docks! This you of course will have seen in the papers. The "Tuscarora" was waiting for us outside, but the British Frigate "Shannon" lay alongside mounting guard over her. For 2 or 3 days we had fine weather, but after that there was a succession of strong head winds and rough seas. The paddle boxes & water closets were carried off at one sweep. Only once did we beat to quarters, and that was a false alarm. I myself got along pretty well! At the end of the second day I had quite recovered from sea sickness, and there has been no resumption of it since! Certainly at sea you cannot have too much sleep at one spell! What is called watch & watch is kept at night! That is one half the crew in duty from 8 to 12, the 2d from 12 to 4, the 1st again from 4 to 8 & so on, so that, when tired & wet you have turned in, scarcely are you comfortably snoring before it is time to turn out again. The provisions are far from good; it is with great difficulty that I can eat at all! Indeed in every way the life is truly a hard one! I could not have borne it but that I know how judicious is the step I have taken. "Time, Faith Energy" is my motto & by that I shall prosper. One thing I do not forget & that is my devotion to our Blessed Lady. Each night when I take my solitary post at the heel of the [word indecipherable] to keep a lookout, the wind blowing ruthlessly & the spray dashing over me at each moment, I beguile the time by reciting the Litany & my night prayers! This I have not once omitted! Time does not in the least reconcile me to the men in the forecastle! More & more do I detest and loathe them! Blasphemy, theft, debaunching [sic] are their practice & their boast, yet I shall have many droll things to tell you when we all meet again. By all the officers I am treated with the greatest consideration! To one of them I give a lesson in French daily, and to another a lesson in music. A song that I wrote, patriotic of course, has been received with great enthusiasm & they say it shall be published when we reach Charleston. When we were out about a week the Captain gave me an agreeable surprise! The Master at Arms, came into the forecastle one morning & said that the Captain had ordered that Dawson & Lusson, my friend, were to take their "things" into one of the rooms in the Upper Deck and were to remain there. This is our Paradise! A small room with two bunks, tiled stand &c beautifully painted & looking out upon the sea is now ours instead of the den we did inhabit. Now when work is over I can be alone! More than this, one of the Middies told me yesterday that he heard the Capain & 1st Lieutenant speaking about me, when the former declared his determination of doing something for me when we arrive. Upon every side I am told that I may make a fortune in the South if I choose. God grant that I may for your sakes.

For me but little is wanting but I am deeply anxious about the result of the bill & the loan. Until I can know that this has been settled I cannot be happy. Still I have a conviction that all will be well! Believe me I feel now all the little faults that I have committed towards you & if I ever return I hope to make you a better & more dutiful son.

We have only put in here to take coals in case that we are chased. No one will be allowed on shore, so that this must be taken by one of the officers.

Let Mad. Plaisir, Strong, & all the crowd know that you have heard from me! Particularly give my love to William. Tell Tetty to make progress with her music, and to be a good girl! I will not forget her! Many a time I fancy I see her dear little face. Last Sunday we were hoisting coals all day. What a contrast to our quiet Sundays at Isleworth. I hope William will [do] as much as is possible [to] take my place—tell him so!

With an earnest prayer that God may watch over & protect you.

> Believe me dearest
> Yours affectionately
> FRANK DAWSON

NORFOLK, VA. MAY 16. 1862.

My dear Mother,

I know too well that your fond maternal affection has long been looking for a letter from this your errant son; and as weeks have passed on so you and my dear friends may have concluded me to be careless or indifferent. Yet it were not possible to think so if you knew the difficulties that now surround any epistolary communication with the lands beyond the sea! A hundred letters may be written and not one shall be received. The prospect of such a fate attending mine determined me to await what appeared to be a favorable opportunity. This I think I have now found through the agency of a friend at Charleston, S.C. and I earnestly hope that this at least may reach you.

Upon our arrival at Bermuda I wrote to you, and that letter you must have received, while the English papers, "Star" "Telegraph" and the rest of the papers spoiling crew will have informed you. But do not allow my particularly hazardous position to be any more compromised in the failure of the "Nashville" to run the blockade, as upon our arrival at Beaufort, N.C. on the 28 Feb. the vessel was sold to a merchantile firm and the whole of the officers and crew transferred. After leaving Beaufort, N.C. I paid a visit to some relatives of Capt. Pegram in Sussex Co. Va., where I was greeted with as kind and warm a reception as though I had been a loved and trusted kinsman, instead of an unknown "Furriner". I was stationed at Norfolk, Va. You of course have heard of the action between the iron plated "Merrimac" or "Virginia" and the Yankee fleet: I was there! About 3 weeks since I was ordered to New Orleans, but when I reached within ten miles of the City of which I had heard so much, I was compelled to turn back as the City was then being rapidly evacuated by our troops. I then returned here, and await orders. It is probable that in a month or two we may have *no fleet,* if so, of course, I join the army! I may not give you any particulars of our condition, but this is not from any fear of the truth being known in Europe; and you may rest assured that while one of her children has power to wield a sword or pull a trigger, the South will never desist from her struggle against the Northern oppressor. The bitter, bitter hate with which the name of Yankee is received here, and the deep-rooted contempt with which every thing so called is met, would be sufficient proof that the conquest of the Southern Confederacy must be nothing short of annihilation.

You, and all of you, have I fervently trust been happy; and that you may be constantly prosperous is my only anxiety. I would say a great deal more, but I cannot be explicit. Whatever is not written must be understood. Give my fondest love to J.A.R., ask him to think of me still with kindness, and kiss darling little Tetty for her brother. Tell Joey that when I return to England, he may if he wishes join his destiny with mine in the Sunny South. I hope that William and his brother and sisters manage to keep at peace with all men; ask William to see you as often as he can and to be for awhile—Mind I won't allow it altogether—your eldest son. Let all my friends know that you have heard from [me] and the circumstances under which I am writing. Let my dear friend Albert to whom this will be sent read my letters.

Prices are rather high here for moderate people. I have paid matches 5*d* a box; Cloth Cap 24/–; Pocket Hdfs. (common) , 6/– each; shoes 40/ pair; Coffee not to be obtained; tea the same. Yet the finest tobacco is but ⅓ per pound

your affectionate son
F. W. DAWSON
C.S.N.

RICHMOND, VA. JUNE 20. 1862
9 p.m.

My dear Mother:

Letters for you from me are flying around in every quarter of the Confederate States so that some may reach you from the most unexpected source. Here is an instance. I am staying at a very nice boarding house on Franklin St. in this City, where the only other boarders are Miss Hetty Cary the celebrated Baltimore beauty, who is even more beautiful in her noble mind and chivalrous disposition than in her charming face, and her sister—equally amiable, but with rather too great a tendency to expand—together with gallant Commodore Hollins of the C. S. Navy of whose gallant exploits in the South you have of course heard. Few in number are we, but important and of course remarkable. Well at Tea about 1/4 of an hour since Miss Hetty,—the beauty, informed me that she was about to send some letters to Baltimore by a person about to run the blockade, and suggested that I should send an epistle by the same channel, having it posted at Baltimore to go by the regular steamer. There am I then endeavoring to send you a long letter in a short time, and filling up my valuable space with mere nothings, am forgetting to tell you of my past & present prospects.

When on the 7 March last I received my appointment as midshipman the C.S.N., and mounted a gray uniform, with any quantity of buttons, gold lace band &c (the uniform by the way cost $90 or about £18, I thought my career to distinction lay before me and that all would be plain sailing. But soon one sea port after another fell into the enemy's hands and it was evident that the Southern Navy was about to return to its original condition, that of zero! With the approbation then of Capt. Pegram I have resigned my appointment, and intend entering the army. It may be some months before I obtain a commission, if I ever do so, and in the meantime I may be persuaded to accept a civil appointment. Be assured of this! that I am starting but to one end, and have but one object in view, that aim, and that object you know.

If at any time you hear of a vessel leaving England for the South you may simply send letters to me addressed to me care of Mrs. V. Pegram, Franklin St., Richmond. Va. If you have the address of Mr. White of Baltimore, send the letter to him, and ask him to send it on! You can scarcely tell how deeply anxious I am to hear from you.

Now for general news. Foreign intervention upon which so much reliance was unfortunately placed six months since, now appears to be imminent and just at the moment when every Southerner had determined to fight alone his battle, it is probable that some unlooked aid may be at hand. I fear very much that France may place her digit in the Southern broth, and if so you may depend that, although making war for an idea, the price of her help will be more than our Confederacy can afford. Louisiana belonged to France, until it was sold for a consideration by a pampered and dissolute monarch, what so natural as that the Louisianian should desire to return to their first love, and declare by the voice of universal suffrage that France and France alone is the mother of her adoption. The Savoy and Nice comedy played once more with increased skill, a few growling, from John Bull and our Gallic friend would rejoice in the possession of an unsought reward for her disinterested conduct. All the maneuvres are understood, and Southern diplomats are slightly "canny". Never was the Southern spirit higher than it is now, every heart is throbbing fast with enthusiasm, every nerve is braced, and from every corner of the Confederacy flock thousands eager to participate in the great struggle under the shade of Richmond's fair City! We are confident of success and with the blessing of God shall obtain the consummation of our independence!

How fondly I think of the circle of dear ones at home! Although I write not your names individually I think of each and every one! Perhaps Joey will be at home when you receive this; God bless him! and my dear little pet of a sister. New tidings from the manufacture districts are most distressing; what can be the effect upon trade?

In health I am well, not having had a day's sickness since my arrival! Indeed it is sometimes jestingly said that I am the only healthy looking gentleman in Richmond.

Goodbye my dear Mother!

May God's blessing always be with you and the whole of my relations and friends!

FRANCIS W. DAWSON

I may not write C.S.N. after my name now!

RICHMOND, VA.
JULY 1, 1862.

My dear Mother:

To some extent I have at least been able to fulfil the aspirations with which I left England & you, and all my dear friends, will think I am sure, that again I have been doing my best to insure a precipitate flight to the realms of darkness and dental gnashing. Before this reaches you, Europe will have heard the result of the engagement that has been waging here since Thursday last, and you may well feel an interest in its details when you think that in its hottest fight your Prodigal son received the wound that is now confining him to the unenviable position of an invalid. I acted again as a volunteer, with Purcell's Battery, commanded by a very dear friend of mine, Capt. Willie Pegram, and my desire to be a participator in a warm engagement is certainly realized. We were in the very thick of the battle, our battery was stationed in an open field, and alone had to bear the weight of the fire from the Yankee guns, which were so placed that they had a cross-fire upon us during the whole of the time. The carnage was fearful, shot and shell were falling around us, while at each moment some poor fellow would fall, groaning, to the ground, there to lie for hours untended, and uncared for. I saw one shell explode and kill three horses and one man, besides cutting off the arm and leg of another unfortunate soldier. At my gun, there were but Capt. Pegram, myself, and two men, instead of the complement of ten. But figures are here more eloquent than words! The official list of casualties in our battery—shows, 4 killed, and 43 wounded, out of about 75 who went into the engagement.

Early in the fight I was knocked down by a fragment of shell, and, when I succeeded in rising to my feet, I found that it had passed in at one side of my pants and out at the other, cutting a hole about 4 inches in length by 1 in. deep in the back of my leg, immediately below the knee. I at once tied my handkerchief around the wound, and went again into action, where I remained until the close at about 9 p.m. After this I had to walk 7 miles into Richmond before obtaining medical aid. This has very much inflamed my wound, and it will be 5 or 6 weeks before I am again convalescent. There is absolutely no danger! And in a day or two I am going down into the country, there to remain until my recovery. Of my conduct I do not wish to speak, but the "Richmond Dispatch" of yesterday, after giving the casualties referred to, has the following paragraph.

"No list proves the desperate bravery, exhibited by the command in the bloody strife. We learn that Mr. Dawson, a young Englishman who came over in the "Nashville", volunteered for the engagement, and received a wound while acting most gallantly."

You will not say that I have disgraced you! In my last letters I explained why I had resigned my appointment in the Navy, and that micawber-like I was waiting for something to turn up! Doubtless something would have turned up had I not been wounded. However I am looked upon as a miniature Achilles! The fairest ladies in Richmond are kind enough to send almost daily inquiring after my health, and deluging me with material tokens of sympathy. Yesterday, Commodore Hollins, Commodore Forrest, and Capt. Sinclair of the Navy were with me. My dear friend Capt. Pegram is a constant visitor.

When you write send your letters under cover to Mr. White at Baltimore, and ask him to take some safe opportunity of sending them on. Direct to me in care of Mrs. Virginia Pegram, Richmond, Va. Your health is I fervently trust better, and also that of all those dear ones at home. I suppose Joey is with you now.

Believe me
My darling Parent
Your affectionate Son
F. W. DAWSON

STONEY CREEK, VA.
AUGUST 3. 1862.

My dear Mother,

My last letters informing you of my participation in the Battle of Richmond have I hope reached you long ere this. I know, my dear Parents what your anxiety must be about me, when in the journals you read the description of the fearful loss of life in each of the engagements by which our Confederacy is fighting its way to freedom; still with the protection of God my life will be spared to cheer and comfort your declining years! This is my constant hope and prayer!

As you know I went to the battle as a volunteer in a battery commanded by my friend Willie Pegram, the carnage was fearful, 69 men were killed and wounded out of about 85. I was struck by a fragment of shell that barely missed the femoral artery. It was a narrow escape. I returned to Richmond, and a month ago moved to the house of a friend in Petersburg, where I remained until last Sunday, when I came down here to recruit my health amid the cotton, corn, and tobacco fields of the Southern States. I am nearly well, and shall return to Richmond in a few days.

The blessing of the Almighty has indeed been upon me since I reached this country. My conduct in action caused the commander of the battery to write me a letter of thanks, and the principal Richmond paper published a higher eulogium of my conduct than I deserved. More than this, Mother, I yesterday received a notification from the Secretary of War, that in consideration of my gallant conduct I had been appointed to the position of first lieutenant of artillery! Do you not feel proud that I have been so honored? How many years must a man serve before he can obtain such a position in the British Army! It is only 3 months and a few days since I landed in this country! I was at once appointed an officer in the navy, resigned this, and now hold a higher [and] better rank in the Army. What a happy moment it will be when, the war concluded, I may visit England, and with my "blushing honors thick upon me" tell you the tale of my perils in "the imminent and deadly breach", describing to you all the "pomp pride and circumstance" of glorious war. I only hope that I may not have to "shoulder my crutch" and show how the field was won, yet when so many are maimed and killed around me how can I hope to escape altogether unscathed? When I reach Richmond I will have my portrait taken for you, and if I am killed it shall be sent to you as soon as it may be done safely. Should I fall, Mother, you will have the consolation of knowing that I die in the communion of the Holy Catholic Church, and we may all look forward with humble confidence to a joyous meeting in Heaven! God bless you all! How dear you are to me now, none can tell! My space is very limited as this will be enclosed to Charleston for transmission, and I fervently trust it may reach you.

Give my love to all my friends and tell them of my success! Kiss dear Teresa for me! Will not Willie be surprised that his boy nephew should be one who like the centurion of old, sayeth to his men Go! and they go; Come! and they come!

P.S. Do not be deceived by the name of Dawson, it is a common one in Georgia, but watch always for Francis Warrington Dawson. Lieut. Artillery.

Ever your affectionate Son
F. W. DAWSON

RICHMOND, VA. AUG. 13. 1862.

My dear WHITNEY,

I arrived here on Monday evening, having perfectly recovered from my wound, & I assure you that I feel physically able again to cope with any one Yankee that the North can produce. This morning I had an interview with Genl. Randolph, and I am appointed brigade ordnance officer in Genl. Longstreet's Division. I leave in the morning and am full of business. When I reach "Old Stonewall" you will I hope hear of, or from, me.

Your kind letter, my dear fellow, was as welcome as a ton of ice and I heartily thank you for your kind consideration in writing to my Mother. Whenever you have any news of me, and can find an opportunity, send a few words to her for me. I feel that I can ask this highest act of friendship from you, without fearing to encroach on your indulgence.

Pray, express to Ingraham, Thomas, Hamilton my high appreciation of their sympathies and congratulations; and assure them on my part that I shall always look back with the most pleasureable feelings to the event that caused me to make their acquaintance. Wherever they may be, I shall always feel the greatest interest in their prosperity and welfare.

Give my warmest regards to your brother &

Believe me

Forever Your Friend

F. W. DAWSON

Fort Delaware, Pa. [Md.]

Sept. 24, 1862.

My dear ALBERT.

I have fallen into tribulation and am now a captive in the tents of the enemy. On the 15 ulto, I left Richmond on Genl. Longstreet's staff and was present at the battle of Manassas, escaping once more unhurt. On the 15 inst. I was ordered to proceed with a train of ordnance waggons to Williams Port, Md. I had no guard whatever, and about a mile from my destination I fell in with a body of 2000 United States Cavalry who were waiting quietly in a corner of the woods. Imagine the result! I was instantly surrounded and ordered to surrender. I did so, my wagons were taken, and I am here. This has been a rather unlucky trip for me. All horses taken are of course confiscated, and I lost two of mine, each worth about £40. All my clothing and equipment are likewise gone. Still it is but the fortune of war; and when I am again at liberty I can soon refit. Our treatment here is good upon the whole, but we suffer from want of exercise. We are at a fort in the middle of the Delaware river and about 90 miles from Philadelphia.

What a contrast old fellow with the many times we had when I was in Europe is this peeping through bars. However qu' importe', as well this way as another. Your health is now I hope completely restored! It was too strange. You in Africa, and I again in America. When the war is over you must come and pay me a visit; if I find it impossible to go and see you all.

Send this letter to Reeks and assure her and all of them of my undiminished affection. You, and your worthy parents will I know believe in the continuance of my warmest friendship.

I cannot write any more now, all our letters are read, and we are limited to two pages. Good bye then once more! In a week or so I will write again.

Believe me always

Your sincere friend

F. W. DAWSON

Lieut. Artillery

[P.S.] We have just been notified that we are to be immediately exchanged!

PETERSBURG, VA. NOV. 22, 1862.

Dearest Mother.

Once again I have reached Confederate soil, and, although my captivity was anything but pleasant, I do not regret it inasmuch as I was enabled to write to you with some prospect of my letters being received. Unless the Yankee officials were more mendacious than usual you have before this received the two letters I sent you from that delectable den of misery Fort Delaware. After about a month's confinement and enduring every indignity that malice and cowardice could contrive, I was paroled and returned to Richmond. I am now fully exchanged and am at liberty to return to duty, which I shall do in a few days. As I cannot tell which of my letters you have received I do not know whether you are aware of the position I now hold. My rank then is first lieutenant of artillery and I am acting as ordnance officer on Gen. Longstreet's Staff. I am proud to tell you that I received my commission for my conduct in the Battle of Richmond where I was severely wounded below the knee by a fragment of shell. My duties are not very onerous and I am perfectly satisfied with my office. The pay is about £20 per month, and were it not for the high prices caused by the War I could hold on very comfortably. Still, of what is £240 per annum, when a cloth coat costs £18, a pair of trousers £7, a waistcoat £3, a pair of shoes £6, a cloth cap £2, a shirt £2 in common calico, a pair of socks 4/.; this is pretty, is it not. Then butter is 8/– a pound; beef 1/6; chickens 5/; turkey £3 each; lucifer matches 2/– and 3/– for a small box; ink 1/ for half a bottle; blacking 9/– a cake; writing paper 8/– a quire, and so on in proportion. I think you will agree with me that this exceeds any thing in California or Australia in their palmiest days. How then is a poor body to exist? Since I have been an officer, now about three months, I have had to purchase two horses and two complete sets of equipment, one having been confiscated by the *infidel Yankees*. The whole cost of these has been about £160, and I have not as yet drawn one cent of pay. You will ask me how this has been done!—honorably, Mother! On my first visit to see Capt. Pegram's family in Sussex Co[unt]y I was introduced to a gentleman named Raines, who has two large plantations in the neighborhood. Do not forget the name Mother, but think of him always as one who has indeed been a father to me. When I met him he for some unaccountable reason took a fancy to me, and soon after I received a letter from him in which, in homely but heartfelt language, he said, "my dollars and cents I will divide with you; half my bread and meat is yours." This noble promise he has nobly fulfilled. His purse has been ever at my command, and without him I could not have accepted the commission offered me. It is not a burden to me as it was understood from the commencement that it was a free gift. I would not have incurred the risk of receiving a loan which I might never be able to repay. His house has been my house, and whenever I can leave the army, I go there to receive the welcome of a beloved son or brother. I have indeed many, many, reasons to thank Providence for his kindness to me! I have acquired dear friends on every side, friends whom I will never forget while life lasts.

It might interest you to form some idea of your Confederate son's present appearance, and I will endeavour to give you some idea. My coat is blue grey, with scarlet cuffs and collars, embroidered with a filigree of gold lace from the wrist to above the elbow, and with two gold bars on the collar to denote my rank, buttons of course in profusion. The pantaloons are of the same texture as the coat, with a broad red stripe at the seams. My cap is the shape of the French kepi; (Albert will describe it to you) the top and sides scarlet and the band black; the whole embroidered with lace in the same style as the coat sleeve. About a week since I purchased a very handsome black horse, he is gaily caparisoned and if you were to see me prancing along on my way about the country you would indeed think me somebody. A military life suits me perfectly although we have to undergo many hardships. Want of sleep and want of food one soon becomes accustomed to; and I soon learned to sleep sounder wrapped up in a blanket, on the bare ground, than I ever did in my own room at home. I have been through some service. I was aboard a vessel of the fleet when the "Merrimac" made her celebrated excursion; I was present at the evacuation of New Orleans, I fought at the Battle of Seven Pines (or Fair Oaks as the Yanks call it) on the 30th April [31 May]; then at the Battles of Richmond from the 26th June to the 4th July where I was wounded, then I was engaged in the [second] Battle of Manassas and since then at the Battle of South Mountain in Maryland after which I was taken prisoner.

During the time that I was recovering from my wound I remained at the house of a relative of Capt. Pegram's in this city, and where indeed I am now staying, and that I have suffered no ill consequences from my wound can only be attributed to the watchful care that attended me from the beginning to the end of my confinement. I was nursed by a niece of Capt. Pegram; and never could a sister have lavished more devoted care on a cherished brother than I received at her hands. Constantly striving to anticipate my lightest wish, cheering me in my moments of pain, and beguiling the long days by her sweet conversation until they seemed but hours, the tide of my existence flowed widely along until I learned to believe that my misfortune had become indeed a blessing. This lady is a belle, not in the ordinary acceptation of the word but she is beautiful in her form, and beautiful in her mind. Every day as you know her more you discover some new trait of character, some new charm of expression, some new cadence in her sweet silvery voice. All who know her love her; and perforce I must do the same. I so wish that I could describe her to you, but my powers would be utterly inadequate to the pleasant task. Petite in form and only sufficiently tall to be perfectly symmetrical, her figure is matured to the rounded lines of womanhood, while in her face redolent with the choicest beauties of expressive action she seems as though girlhood had scarcely been attained. Loving brown eyes, perfect hands and a rich mass of glorious auburn hair, real auburn, mind, render her such as dreamers may have fancied but such as I have never seen before. You will think me partial, but it is not so. Even take from her every personal charm and she would be more beautiful then than any you have met. Her pure, though brilliant mind, shining through her eyes would impart to her a loveliness that mere bodily symmetry can never know. Flattered and caressed from childhood, followed by the adulation of the world, she has never been spoiled, & now lives, the sunshine of those whom she loves, the perfection of the Creator's work, a loving, trusting woman.

I received your letter written when you had heard of my arrival at Beaufort. I did not receive it until about a month since, and the news was very old. Please give my warmest thanks to Mrs. Allen for her kindness. I am anxious to have some late news from you to know how you are all getting on. It is much more difficult I know for you to send a letter here than it is for me to write to you, still you may have opportunities occasionally, through Mrs. Allen and Dr. Smith. Whenever I can find a favorable moment I will have my likeness taken to be sent to you. Remember me to all my friends. I address my letters always to Albert's care for a reason that his address is not likely to be changed & for reasons connected with myself which I cannot explain until I know that my letter[s] will remain unread until they reach their destination.

Give my warmest love to Sister Tetty, tell her not to forget me, and one day if you will permit she shall come to see her brother in Virginia. Joseph is still I suppose at school. Tell him to be diligent in his studies while he has it in his power. Give my warmest love to the Governor; and William, & every body else generally, & believe me I remain though so far distant

Your devoted Son
F. W. DAWSON

HEAD QUARTERS DEPARTMENT VIRGINIA AND N. CAROLINA
PETERSBURG VA. APRIL 23. 1863.
My dear Mother,

Yesterday I had the pleasure of receiving a letter from my friend Whitney enclosing two letters from you and one from David, and it would be impossible for me to tell you how overjoyed I am to find you and all well and comparatively happy. I had had but one letter from you before then and that was dated in March 1862 and telling me that you had heard of our safe arrival. Month after month had passed and still I had no news, and I had almost been forced into the conviction that you had not written. Every one had been receiving letters from England but me and I was deeply grieved and disappointed. For this reason and no other I have not written home during the past three months, now however you know how to send your letters and I shall expect that either you or the Governor will write to me once a month. I will do the same and we shall then be sure to hear of each other pretty frequently. I thank you so much, dear Mother, for Joey's likeness, don't forget to send me also Theresa's. Your last news of me was from *that den of thieves Fort Delaware. As you may imagine I could not write to you freely as all our* letters were examined. We were treated with the greatest hardship and ignominy half starved; ninety officers were packed into a room about 30 ft x 20 ft and we were not allowed to leave its filthy precincts for any purpose night or day. Three days after my last letter to you we were paroled and sent in a steamer up the James River to a point near Richmond; we were four days on the trip and had but two scanty meals during the whole time. I never felt more unmixed joy than when my feet were once more planted on Southern soil. I stayed a few days in Richmond and then went down to my adopted home in Sussex County where I was received with open arms and the warmest greeting: every one had thought me killed, and Capt. Pegram particularly was in great anxiety and distress. However the Prodigal son returned and the fatted veal was slaughtered incontinently. I was in a lamentable condition, all my worldly property was on my back and I was compelled to obtain an entire new outfit, which in the present condition of our sweet Confederacy cost now nearly $1,000 or £200. A week or two placed me again in marching order and I started off to join Genl. Longstreet at Fredericksburg. The Army under the Command of Genl. Robt. E. Lee was composed of two corps the 1st command by Longstreet and the 2nd by General Jackson. Our position was a magnificent one and the skill of our engineers had been taxed to the utmost to render it impregnable. Of course you read of Burnside's attack on us and of his ignominious defeat. Never in my life do I expect to see such a magnificent sight again. From the crest of a hill where I was stationed with Lee, Longstreet, Pickett, Stuart, and others of our principal generals the whole scene of conflict was before our eyes, and at our feet, the glorious sun shining out as tho' bloodshed and slaughter were unknown on the beautiful earth; the screaming of shells and the singing of rifle bullets adding a fearful accompaniment to the continued booming of the heavy guns. In God's mercy I was again spared, altho' at one time I was in a group with three other officers each of whom was struck at the same moment; I alone escaped. This is the 7th pitched battle in which I have been engaged, and I hope before the War closes to extend my roll of honor. After the battles of Fredericksburg matters remained quiet for a while and then there being the expectation of an advanced [sic] by the enemy Gen Longstreet was sent with the corps away from Fredericksburg, and was directed to assume command of the Department of Virginia and North Carolina. Petersburg is our present headquarters but I hope soon to be in the field again, and to remain there until the last cowardly Yankee has been expelled [from] the sacred soil of Virginia. I think you understand that I am on Genl. Longstreet's staff with the rank of 1st lieut. of artillery and whenever you read in the journals of Longstreet's whereabouts you will know where I am. So much for myself. I was very much gratified to find that the Governor had obtained a position that will be less precarious than one depending alone on commissions, don't let him be too trusting or confiding in Mr. Dawson or any one else, let him know exactly his position and what he is entitled to and demand it to a hair's breadth. You may depend that a man who exacts all that he is entitled to is thought better of than one who allows himself to be talked into any thing that is convenient. The settlement of Spokes' claim ought to be a great relief, and now he will feel himself unshackled. And your health, my dear Mother, is better you tell me. I hope that God will protect and bless you all and preserve you from any danger. You must kiss my dear little sister again and again for me! I know not what my position may be here when the War closes, but it shall be my aim to relieve you of all care and expense so far as she and Joey are concerned. If I am spared I may yet be a comfort and aid to you. William is I suppose in the same position, tell him to write! The more letters you send the better the chance I have of receiving some of them. I shall have constant chances of writing to you, and you had all better address your letters to me at the Post Office Nassau N[ew] P[rovidence] to be left till called for. I have other friends besides Whitney who run the blockade between Charleston and Nassau, and I will get each of them to call for my letters. I have had no letters yet from Albert, tell him that I am very anxious to hear from him; give M & Mad. Plaisir and Albert my warmest regards. I intend next time to write Albert & so on alternately. Be sure when you write to send me Cousin Henry White's address in Baltimore, I have a number of friends in that city and I may be able to hear from him. Ask Albert to find out any news he can of my old flame Miss Botting.

I am very anxious to hear some news of her. Each time that you write let me know if you have any news on this subject, she is a charming girl and I wish that you knew her. Don't be afraid of repeating your news as I may not receive all your letters. You must give my regards for me to Monsg'r Weld [?]. I am deeply sensible of his kindness. Give my warmest love to Father and the children and all my relations. I feel that I have given you but very little news in this letter but in my next I will endeavor to give you some idea of our condition and prospects. We are hopeful and confident and there is no earthly doubt of the ultimate success of the great rebellion. I am very highly thought of here; pardon the apparent egotism of the remark. I have a troop of wealthy and influential friends here who will do anything for me. Mr. Raines of whom I have spoken to you before has even expressed a wish to adopt me as a son. I have no hardship of any consequence to endure, money I can command whenever I require it. Gen. Longstreet even has offered to use his influence to procure me an appointment in the regular army if I wish to remain permanently in the army. My dear friend Capt. Pegram, whom I have to thank for my every success does not wish me to do this, as he thinks I can do much better in a mercantile career. There is plenty of time however to arrange all this. Tell David not to think of going to New Zealand. This country will be the finest opening in the world, and if he wishes to come out here when the War is over I can assist him to a position here that will pay him much better and be more pleasant. I send you a paragraph from one of the leading Richmond papers which may interest you, keep it in remembrance of your absent son. Whenever I have an opportunity of doing so I will send you my likeness in full uniform; one of these days I may astonish the citizens of London by parading Regent St. in full-gorgeousness of gray, scarlet, and gold lace. Once more my fondest love to you and my father and brother and sister and Believe me Your affectionate son

FRANCIS W. DAWSON

P.S.   I suffer no inconvenience from my old wound now! You had better continue to address your letters as Mr. Whitney directed he knows the route much better than I do.

FWD

HEAD QUARTERS 1 CORP, A.N. VA.
SEPT. 5, 1863

Dearest Mother;

I send this letter through flag of truce and the space allowed is limited: excuse the brevity. A few days since I recd your letter of June 15; I was very anxious as the last previous letter was only January. Thank God! that your health is so much better, think of me always, dear Mother, and ask all my dear friends to do the same. Tell them they can not better prove their regard than by writing. I have already told you how to send your letters, continue to address them, when you send directly to me at Richmond. Let me know all the news from home, any thing about any one that I know will interest and please me. What has Strong been doing to bring him into so much disrepute? Nothing very bad I hope. Thank Bartley for his kind message, tell him I shall have some yarns that will astonish him if we meet again; material enough for a dozen five act romance dramas had I not gotten over that foolish mania. If I had all my paper spoilings here I might convince the Southerners that I was not so foolish in England as I am here perhaps! Don't forget about my old Lady Love, altho' I suppose I am forgotten as she deserved to be. Tell me about her each time you write, and I shall be sure to receive some of them. Give Wm. and the Gov. my love and tell them they can not know how earnestly I wish them happiness & prosperity. I am perfectly well, and escaped unhurt at Gettysburg; it was a warm place though. I hold the same rank as first lieut. of artillery on Gen. Longstreet's staff. In the artillery promotion is very slow, but the Gen. promised me promotion before long. I should like to give you all my domestic details, but I must await a better opportunity. I have everything here to make me happy save you and my dear family. God bless them! My position is one that causes me to be well known over the entire army: and I think I may say that I have reflected no discredit on myself or you. Remember me to everybody I have not space to write their names. Kiss my brother & sister for me & remember me always in your prayers.

Your affectionate Child
FRANCIS W. DAWSON

HEAD QUARTERS LONGSTREET'S CORPS, N. CHATTANOOGA, TENN.
SEPT. 29. 1863

My dear Mother:

There is a flag of truce today for the purpose of passing the wounded prisoners through the lines and I may be able to send this to you. As you will see by the superscriptions we have moved our quarters from Virginia to Tennessee and so far as I am concerned the change is anything but agreeable; the weather is very cold at night and particularly damp, provocative of all kinds of chills and rheumatisms but fortunately I have not been unwell since I reached this country. I particularly wish you to write whenever you can find an opportunity as I am always anxious to hear from you and so many letters miscarry that certainly not more than half your letters will probably be received. Last night I was dreaming of you and it makes me feel very sad to be here entirely alone. In Virginia, I have dear and fine friends but in this desolate state I know no one and I feel very lonely. I wonder whether you ever take a map and trace out the movements of the armies to see where I am, you might easily do so; Longstreet's name must be frequently mentioned in the papers & wherever he is there am I; it will be a consolation to me to feel even that you are doing this. I hope that before this you have sent Joseph to college, I wish heartily that I could be of any assistance, tell him to be a good boy and as soon as the War is over I will go home to see you all. Kiss dear Sis for me tell her to be a good girl and not to forget me. Give my love to the Govn. and William. I have met several English officers here but none whom I knew in England, Mr. Vizitelli the correspondent of the Illustrated News slept in my tent last night. All the notabilites come to our headquarters and of course I see them all, this is one great source of pleasure to me. Col. Manning, chief of ordnance of Longstreet's Army was wounded on Sunday and the whole care and responsibility rests upon me; I have indeed as much anxiety as as I can well bear. Write to me to the same address as before. Your affectionate Son

FRANCIS W. DAWSON

HEAD QUARTERS 1 CORPS, A.N. VA.
NEAR RICHMOND, VA., JUNE 1, 1864

My dear, dear, Mother;

While I was at Abingdon Va, on the Tennessee R.R. between Lynchburg and Bristol, late in April I received a package of letters from you dated November last. It is true that they were rather old, but then there were so many of them that I had news of every description. Thank David, Aunt Sarah, William & Mad. Plaisir for their considerate kindness, I am delighted that David is prospering so well in his profession; he deserves to succeed. I am not very old it is true, but, during the last two years, I have twice risen, unaided by outside influence, from the position of a private to that of a commissioned officer, and I am confident that zeal, integrity, honor, and a little practice, must command success in any undertaking. My dear friend Albert is still among the clouted Moors, and, like Daniel, is in the den of lions although not so unpleasantly close as was our friend the prophet. Mad. Plaisir's affectionate letter was a jewel! To you and my dear, kind, father, ordinary words of thanks would be but faint praise. I can find words to thank all but you! Here, amid the perils of war, the scream of the shell and the crack of the sharpshooter's musket even now echoing in my ear, I feel how much I have sinned against your tender care and loving kindness! Forgive me, my dear Parents, every unkind word and harsh thought, and believe that in my heart

I am, as always, your affectionate child. Pray always for me, you can not know the fearful and deadly perils I have escaped, and the Good God may have shielded me in answer to your supplications. You have seen that our first chief Gen. Longstreet was wounded by our own men, this was my narrowest escape. There were but about eight of us together, all mounted, Gen. Longstreet and four of his staff officers including myself, Gen. Jenkins, a Capt. Dwight and a Capt. Dobie. *Without a moments warning* one of our brigades about 2,000 *strong*, only 50 or 60 yards distants [*sic*] poured a deliberate fire into us. Longstreet was badly wounded, Gen. Jenkins, Capt. Dwight & Dobie killed on the spot: I was not even scratched. Again and again has God spared me and it can only be in response to your prayers.

Thank Goodness we have left Tennessee and are back in "Ole Virginny" with Gen. Lee, our Corps arriving in time as usual to change the fate of battle at Wilderness Run, and to take a hand at Spottsylvania C.H. We are now in front of Richmond again expecting a repetition of the Seven Days fight, I should not mind being hit, or getting a furlough wound, as we call them, as I have not had a leave of absence for nearly twelve months. Give Joe a kiss for his letter and tell him that I bought a beautiful young cream colored horse, with a long mane and tail, the other day, which I should like him to have if he would come and get him. I would give anything to have Brother here, he would make an admirable courier. Dear little Sister too, I wonder whether I shall ever see her again? Please God however I will, as we are going to whip Old Grant out of his boots in a few days and I don't think that even the Yanks can stand the "Rebellion" much longer. Brother says in his letter that you only want £50 and me to make you happy. Now if Confederate money were as good as gold you could have twice £50 by asking me for it, but unfortunately our currency is so much depreciated that £1 in gold will buy £20 in Confederate money. My pay is $140 or £28 a month but in gold this would only be a little more than £1. Of course this estimate is to a great extent fallacious as although it takes $20 Confederate to buy $1 in gold, the Confederate $20 will buy far more than the gold $1. The cause is not so much the depreciation of the currency as a scarcity of gold. However when peace returns I suppose our money will improve and you can then have the £50 by the first steamer if you want it. Gigantic fortunes have been made here since the War, and I could have done the same as others had I wished to shirk my duty—I am better satisfied as it is, I have the friendship of many of the first men in the country, and if I wish to go into trade after the War I can command any assistance that I may need. I wrote Albert a long letter from Jonesborough which [I] hope has been received. From the irregularity in receiving your letters I am convinced that you do not send them in the proper way. Address them to me in an envelope addressed Major Norman Walker, Bermuda, and request him to send them on, this is a sure channel. I was rather amused at David's account of his cramming for examination and the more especially as I had just stood one myself of a far different character. My examination included plane and spherical trigonometry, algebra, mechanics & chemistry, all more particularly as applied, to the

laws and composition of projectiles, and the science of war. I am happy
to say that I passed with high honors, and although there was no vacancy,
I was promoted on the 2 April 1864 to a *captaincy*. You remember the
likeness I promised you, I had one taken but it is very mean, so I will
have another taken in captain's uniform and endeavor to send you a
copy at the same time that this letter goes. My friend Capt. Sinclair of
the Navy has promised to take charge of this; we are only four miles
from Richmond, but I am continually in the saddle and cannot get away
as we are expecting a general engagement. It must be rather surprising to you to hear me speak of *horses* and *riding* when you know that
until I left home I had never been in the saddle in my life; but in sober
truth the saddle is the headquarters of a staff officer and by dint of long
practice you cannot fail, however stupid, to become moderately expert.
Do not either distress yourself by thinking that I have now to endure
many hardships. A staff officer has many privileges, I am in splendid
health and enjoy thoroughly my adventurous existence. We live on ½ lb.
of bacon and 1 lb flour a day and find that it is ample, if we had but a
little variety; we sleep in a blanket under a tree or a tent and are su-
premely well in health and spirits. The most amusing thing however is
the high prices in town. I paid a negro the other day £1. for blacking my
boots; is it not absurd? By all means read the Southern Correspondence
published in the "Morning Herald", the same letters are published in
one of our Richmond papers. The letters are good as a whole but contain many little inaccuracies. In his account of the Battle of the Wilderness he says that Gen. Longstreet was lifted from his horse by Maj. Walton of his staff when he was shot. Walton was not within *two miles* of
the place at the time. Gen. Longstreet weighs over 200 lbs. and he was
lifted from his horse by Col. Sorrel, Col. Manning and myself.

Thank my dear father many many times, for his letter, and its warm
expressions of Southern feeling, tell him to work on in the good cause;
I could open the eyes of the Abolitionists in England if I had the opportunity. Tell father to write me more about himself, as that interests
me most of all. You know the purity of my motive in changing my name
when I left England! I wish that I had not done so as it may cause me
hereafter some annoyance, but I have won everything that is honorable
in my life under my present name and to that I must for ever adhere.
My idea was that Uncle Dawson had always been so affectionate to me,
that in assuming his name I might assume him, and one of my greatest
prides has been the knowledge that my uncle was in the English Army
and killed in India. I have spoken of him, and of myself, *to one person
only* and I told him that I was *adopted* and *changed my name;* but that
thank God my own dear father is still living to bless his wandering son.
I tell you this in order to place you on your guard in case you should
meet any of our officers in England who know me, and who of course
would be immediately struck by the difference of name. Give my warmest love to everybody, particularly father and brother and sister and
William and everybody generally, tell them all to *write, write, write!*
Address Capt. F.W. Dawson, Gen. Longstreet's staff. Headquarters and
Corps, A.N. Va., enclosed to Maj. Walker.

God bless you dear Mother and Good: bye. (See my official signature!) *Greek is it not?*

FRANCIS W. DAWSON
Capt & Asst. Chf. Ord.
1 Corps A.N. Va.

P.S. My regards to Mr & Mrs Sleet & Msgr Weld & why on earth did you not find out about *my sweetheart* as I asked you to do, I shall have to come over all gold lace and spurs if you don't.

HEAD QUARTERS 1 CORPS, A.N. VA.
PETERSBURG JUNE 26 1864

My dear, dear, Mother:

Little did I think when years ago I saw drawings and sketches in the Illustrated by our "special artist F. Vizetelli", or even when we had many a frolic together in the mountains of Tennessee, that he the same joyous corpulent artist would have proved a source of such happiness to my dear parents and to myself. He arrived a few days ago from Europe and brought me your letter of April 27, the last which I had were those sent by Mr. Ward I think, at all events there was a whole budget of them there from Mad. Plaisir, David and the rest. This time I had but yours, and I was greviously [sic] disappointed that father did not write to his son, the captain: I suppose however that the dear patriarch did not know you were able to send by so sure a channel. I am heartily glad that Vizetelli was able to communicate with Cousin White as you have been thus incontestably assured that in this country I have led in my profession an honorable life. The great mystery to me is that I have done so well, and I am at least half inclined to believe that William's often repeated assertions of confidence in my future were not the mere partial praises I then took them to be. However it may be I am captain now and in a month or two I have nearly the certainty of being again promoted. It will be a welcome moment and a happy one when this little difficulty of ours is over and I am enabled to see you all again, and startle sister's eyes with my Confederate uniform and big sabre. A military career cannot be profitable in a pecuniary sense, but the time is passing away, & at the close of the War I shall be no more poorer in pocket than when I began while I shall be enriched in experience and the conscious possession of many dear friends. My worldly possessions fluctuate considerably, a week or two since my wordly possessions here were worth, horses and one thing and another, $6,000, or about £1200; but the Yankees made a raid through here and carried off my finest horse from Mr. Raines' and then I lost at one jump more than $3,000, or £600. Mr. Raines lost at least twenty thousand pounds by the same raid, but he is very wealthy, and is content to give up every cent to secure our country's success. He has two daughters, both charming girls, and I might be tempted one of these days, but at present thank goodness I am sound in my "youthful affections". Since Gen. Longstreet was wounded Gen. Anderson has commanded our corps, but you must continue to address as before, as Gen. Longstreet will soon return to duty. You have heard of course of our fights with Grant, and it is very amusing to us as it cannot be to you, to read the mendacious accounts of the Yankee papers. Grant is now trying to take Petersburg and we are here to have a word or two in the matter, yet yesterday I read an account from a New York paper of the *capture* and *occupation* of *Petersburg*. Judging by all generous standards England has behaved very shabbily towards us, but thank God she seems to be prosperous, and we don't care for her assistance one straw. We can do without her aid and only ask that no unfair advantage may be given our enemies. The atrocities committed by the Yanks cannot be known to you, their raiding parties pass through the land, carry off all the slaves, destroy all provisions, break up the farming tools, drive off the horses and mules, insult in the *grossest manner* the poor women whom they meet, and then shoot or hang a father or brother for daring to interfere. Even now their negro troops bayonet the wounded men who are left on the field, a man came in yesterday who made his escape and who makes oath that he saw this done only a day or two ago. But I don't feel like writing about the War as I hear and see quite enough of it in every shape. My health is glorious, I have not been sick a week yet, although we are exposed with no shelter but a tent to the almost tropical heat of summer, and the rigors of winter. I wrote you a long letter by Capt. Sinclair a week or two ago, and I have written about once a month. There is no difficulty at all in your writing, vessels come in every day nearly and Major Walker C.S.A. Bermuda will send on my letters if you mention my rank and position. I am surprised that you should have seen Miss Allen and understood that you looked upon them very cooly [sic]; I on the other hand have always retained the warmest appreciation of their kindness and never forget a friend, particularly now. You must give all the necessary kind messages to my friends, and make allowances for the difficulties under which I labor in writing at all. There are but very few Englishmen of any note in our service, Capt. S. Winthrop (a Wiltshire family) has gained a very high reputation for distinguished and conspicuous gallantry which in the English service would have gained him the Victoria Cross; then there is Col. Fielding who is with Beauregard and one or two others. There seems to be no jealousy concerning us, and we are placed on the same footing as Southerners born which is all that we ask. I am heartily pleased that Joe has gone to college, although I am not altogether pleased that he should study for the ministry. Give him youth, energy, and education, and in this country he could soon make a fortune and place you all in affluence. I am too old and indolent, but I am going to "look around" after the War and see if anything will turn up. The best chance will be at the cessation of hostilities, but I must try and get home first and come to the "filthy lucre" afterwards. I had my likeness taken the other day but it is too bad to send you, and I must try again. I shall have some carte de visites taken so that I may send over two or three to you. In the meantime you may figure me to yourself as unchanged. I look as stupidly boyish as ever and cannot raise a moustach under any provocation, the only change is that I am as brown as mahogany in face and hands, and have several unpleasant holes in my socks and missing buttons which never troubled me at home. I am like the man who never knew that clothes wore out or buttons came off, until he left home and had to be his own awkward tailor. I am very glad that you are so intimate with the Plaisirs; I count them among my dearest friends and Albert has always been to me as a brother; give him my warmest love if he is in England and ask him to write. How is Andrew your favorite getting on, is he not agent for something or other? London must be mighty hot if it is anything like this place. I am in a writing mood and hardly know what I am about. Send me the address of your cousin Mr. White of Baltimore as I may be taken prisoner, and he would then be invaluable; also let me know whether you have heard any thing of my friends John and Fred Hasken [?] you never liked them but they were true as steel to us. Tell father to keep up his courage, he ought to be glad that such an encumbrance as myself is off his hands, and yet I know that he wants me back again; it seems to me that I would give anything to be back with you for a few hours. Take care however, when I do come back it will be like a thief in the night, & I shall have so much to tell that there will be no sleep for a night or two. Goodbye dear Mother, always pray for me or I shall not live to see you once again. Kiss father & sister for me and brother when you see him. Tell Father to write me about himself. I don't know half enough about you.

Your affectionate child
FRANCIS W. DAWSON

P.S. I have to write my name so many times a day that it becomes gradually more undistinguishable.

RICHMOND, VA., AUG. 7, 1864

My dear, dear Mother

We have just come over from Petersburg where we have been stationed some time and you may imagine my pleasure when I found at Mrs. Pegram's a letter from you. Our whole corps leaves here tonight on the train to reinforce Gen. Early in the Valley and I am now striving to write you a few lines and answer all your queries. I am well, thoroughly well, weigh about 160 lbs, and want for nothing, I live well all the time and rejoice daily in things that in England would be termed luxuries, we have melons and peaches in profusion but in camp of course our principal diet is "bacon with bread", which I despise. I have everything which is necessary, an abundance of clothes and comforts of every kind, good horses to ride and a good servant. Most of the things necessary for us we obtain from the gov't at about one tenth of market rates and this it is which enables us to get along so well. I have received my commission as captain dating from April 2, 1864. I have written to you three times in the last month, your letters by Col. Ward and by my friend Vizetelli, have been received. My pay is now £30 per month, if it were only in gold I could soon relieve you from your difficulties. Have I in any way offended father, that he does not write. Night and day I sympathise with you and feel ashamed that I am not with you to share your trouble although in England I can do nothing. This country is my only hope. There will be immense trade as soon as the war closes and that will be my opportunity but if you think that I can assist you I will be home by the first steamer after the War. Write to me freely and under your own name. I have told people here that I was adopted by my uncle to settle my change of name as by my present name I must now stand or fall. I have had no letter from Albert or from Bartley; none from other than yourself except those sent by Mr. Ward. I am deeply grieved that father is so unsuccessful. I know that he does all in his power but fortune is against him as it once was against me. My friend Mr. Raines is well; the Yanks went near his plantation on their last raid and stole about £20,000. worth of negroes, he is now in Mecklenburg with his family. I spent a leave of 15 days there and only returned a few days ago.

I have left your address with my friends so that you may be written to if I am killed; we are starting on a fresh campaign now and I don't know what the result may be. I had my likeness today taken; I have sent to my quarters for a copy; it will be enclosed if it comes in time. I have not black hair in spite of my *"likeness"*, it is wretched so they all say. You think that I must have a great deal to say, but the exciting occurrences of our lives are as quiet to us as your peaceful home at Isleworth. Cheer on Joey and encourage him to study hard, let his profession be what it may this will give him the means of success if he has the *will!* Kiss Tetty for me, dear child, I am very anxious to see her. I send you a specimen of the Yankee small change worth d2½ and one of our dollar bills worth nominally four shillings. The Confederate is rather tattered but like our soldiers it stands well. Send all your letters to Maj. Norman Walker, it is the best means. Mr. Whitney has been taken prisoner, so that all your Nassau letters are lost to me. We are about to depart and I must say good bye. Give my love to father and every body generally.

Believe me I remain
Your affectionate Son
FRANCIS W. DAWSON
My official signature *Capt Asst Chf. Ord.*
1 Corp A. N. Va.

HEAD QUARTERS, 1 CORPS A.N. VA.,
NEAR RICHMOND, VA., OCT. 13, 1864

My dear, dear Mother;

We have had a pretty brisk little fight today; Grant has been feeling our lines on this (North) side of the River; he made but two attacks on our ranks and each time was easily repulsed; our loss slight! We left our camp early this morning, and did not return until after dark, when I found that a days fighting and riding as usual had a very healthy effect on my appetite & impelled me to call lustily for dinner. My servant soon confronted me with a broiled chicken and some stewed apples and I was sitting over my fire, dodging the smoke which always will get into your eyes, when a courier brought me a letter. I thought it was some bothering communication on official business and did not care to look at it, but accidentally, dear Mother, I spied your well known writing and found that I had again a pleasure of which I had almost despaired. The last letter I had from you I recd on Aug 6, it was that which you sent when you wrote to Mrs. Pegram. The present letter must have come through Major Walker and, if so, pray continue to write through the same channel, I can bear every thing but silence, however caused, of those whom

I love in England. A word or two on Confederate affairs: Since May 6 when Gen. Longstreet was wounded Gen. Anderson has been commanding our corps, and on Aug. 7 we went up to the valley to reinforce Early. We had some pretty little fighting, and more than once your son thought that the moment had come for him to quit this gay & festive scene, but we at last left our troops with Early, and on Sept. 27, the Gen., Anderson, and ourselves arrived again safe in Richmond. Since that time Gen. Anderson has been in command of all the troops on the North side of the River, under Gen. Lee, while Gen. A. P. Hill commands in the same manner at Petersburg. It would be difficult to explain the position of affairs here unless you know the country well or had a map, but the Times will have told you that Grant has now a tremendous line, his left resting on the R.R. at Petersburg and his right on this side of the River sweeping partly round Richmond. There are croakers everywhere and you must have them in England, but you must not allow any of them to persuade you that we are, as the Yankees say "in our last ditch." The army is in fine spirits, better clad, better fed, and better armed than I have ever before seen it, and if Gen. Lee is only spared we can laugh defiance at Grant and his legions. I am happy to say that Gen. Longstreet reported for duty today, his right arm and hand is still paralysed from his wound but he could not be kept back any longer, and we hope in a day or two to hail him again in command of the I Corps, A.N. Va. He is a tower of strength to our cause, and he returns at good time.

My personal affairs are in some respects not very flourishing. I told you that the Yanks captured one of my horses with £400 last May. I bought a new horse in the Valley for £200, when my beautiful negro servant eloped with him and has not been heard of since. These were serious losses but I must not complain. I have but one horse now in service, but I have a colt that I think will be fit to ride in the Spring and that will help me considerably. Confederate money seems to get worse and worse, it costs £70 for a pair of boots, £3 now for lb. coffee, 44/- for common sugar. I bought some cloth the other day to make a pair of trousers and waistcoat, the making alone will cost £20. A collar costs £1, a pocket hankerchief £2, a newspaper 2/– and tobacco which two years ago was a shilling a lb. now costs £1.15.0. At such absurd rates, which are utterly unwarranted, you may conceive that my £360 per annum does not go very far, but it cannot last long and if I come out safe in limb it is all that I ask. My friend Mr. Raines is as thoughtfully kind as ever. You know he was run off from his plantation by the Yankees and is now staying with his son-in-law Dr. W. H. Jones, Boydton, Mecklenberg Co., Va. From Mr. Raines I can have anything that I ask for, but as you may well imagine this very liberality keeps me from calling upon him, and I will never do so but in a case of urgent necessity. What I value more than money is that I have always a home at his house. I have somewhere to go to if I am sick or wounded and do not feel entirely homeless. When we go into winter quarters, if Grant does not keep us moving all the winter, which the Lord forbid, I shall get a thirty days leave and go to Mecklenberg. I cannot say that I dislike this exciting, adventurous life, but I should like to have regular mails, and Confederate paper as

good as gold. I am perfectly well in health and comparatively contented
in mind; I know that I bear a high reputation as an officer; and more
than all I look forward now with confidence to meeting you all once
more for a time in happy England. I am very glad that Father wrote to
me so fully; I am better satisfied when I know every thing. He must
cheer up, and persevere, wait and hope, put his shoulder to the wheel
as he is doing now and we will all get out of the mire at last. If it is ever
my good fortune to be married, I pray that my wife may be to me all
that you have been to my dear father, you have been a help mate indeed, your patience, courage, and faith only shining the more brightly
when our faith has been shaded by the clouds of adversity. God will bless
you, dear Mother, for your faithful stewardship, a true wife and good
mother; would that I could be with you to share your sorrows and light-
en the burden of your trials. As for William, ("Uncle William" I beg
his pardon) I am sure that he is the same good-working, good-natured,
good-hearted, generous being that he was when I came away; thank him
a thousand times for me, but he requires no thanks, and he can do far
more for you than I could. Give my warmest love to him! From Bartley
I have had no letters. Capt. Winthrop who is over here gets his letters
through the correspondents in Liverpool of Messrs. Fraser, Trenholm &
Co of Charleston. You can write this way, but I think the other the best,
(same way that is as your letter of Aug. 31) . If Joe is a good boy I will
give up all idea of taking him as a courier, perhaps he likes his books
better than bullets and tell him he is quite right. It is much better to
go out of the world in a natural way than by having 1½ lbs of iron or
2 oz. of lead through your body. Has not my fortune been good! I have
only been wounded once, my horse was hit the other day and I have
had some narrow escapes. Have you seen a book by Col. Fremantle entitled "3 months in the Southern States." it may interest you to read
it if you know that I was through the whole of the Gettysburg campaign
which he describes, Gen. Longstreet's staff of whom he speaks are my
daily companions, I was with Gen. L. when Pickett charged. I know Col.
F. slightly, he was wrong in saying that Major Moses discovered a lot of
hats in Chambersburg. I found them in a cellar and fitted out the entire staff from Gen. L. down to myself. Vizetelly always stays near us, and
all his pictures represent scenes in which I have figured; have his views
of Front Royal and the fight at Berryville appeared? I saw them before
they left. You must give my kindest regards to the Plaisirs and ask Mad.
Plaisir to write me a long French letter, tell her I have never had occasion to speak French but once and that was with Felix Beauregard, son
of Gen. Beauregard. Tell Sister Teresa to grow up as pretty as she can
and as good as your example will make her. Kiss her and tell her I am
proud of my little sister and she must be able to play "God save the
Queen" and "In my cottage" by the end of the War. If I have omitted
any one or any thing you must excuse it. I was anxious to write tonight
as today's affair was probably only an introduction and we may have hot
work in the morn. Our hardest fighting will come within the next week
or two; after the 15 November Richmond is safe. I constantly dream that
I am at home and *scared nearly to death at not being able to return*

here before the expiration of my leave. I have arranged that you shall be written to if I am seriously hurt. Any news from Australia?

>   with many kisses and much love to you all
>   I remain your affectionate son
>   FRANCIS D. DAWSON

RICHMOND, VA. NOV. 25. 1864

My Dear Mother:

Surely some of my letters, numerous as they are, will in time reach you, and I myself live in hope that I may ere long hear from you again. The last letter I received was dated Aug 31, I think and came out very rapidly. I have written you twice since it arrived. I am anxious to hear that you have received my likeness which I sent you as I must send you another at once if the first has not reached you. During the last week or two a considerable and important change has been worked in my position. I have been removed from Gen Longstreet's Staff and am now Chief Ordnance Officer on the Staff of Major Gen Fitz Lee (a nephew of Gen R. E. Lee) who commands all the cavalry in the Valley of Virginia. Gen Fitz Lee heard of me through some of our mutual English friends and made application for me, it was a high compliment and he has received me in a manner that all goes well for the comfort and pleasure of our future relations. Tomorrow morning I leave for the valley to join my command & I shall not then have many opportunities of writing to you; I anticipate that we shall have plenty of amusement in fighting during the winter and I shall arrange that you be written to at once if I am seriously hurt at any time. A great deal of kindness has always been extended to me since I have been in this Country, and, although I have suffered but little, it is useless to deny that there is considerable jealousy displayed towards an Englishman. There is already one English Officer, Capt Cavendish (late of the Hussars) on our Staff, and I am determined now to win for myself the respect if not the esteem of even the bitterest enemys of the "old country". To your prayers alone, dear Mother, in the mercy of God do I attribute the immunity from harm which has hitherto attended me, and I pray that I may be spared through this War to have the happiness of meeting you once again; yet, when I think of the many, many noble fellows among my friends who have already fallen, I can scarcely hope to be one of the few to escape. So far my health has been perfectly good, and my privations far less than any one could suppose. Of course the Yanks think they are going to close up up in a very short time, but they know not as we know the pride and power of the South. I believe firmly that the South can continue this War for two years longer, and it will be done at any cost in preference to surrendering that fair land to the tyrannous rule of the North. The ranks of the Army are being rapidly filled, the Army and people are in fine spirits, our supplies of provisions and clothing are abundant, no one thinks or dreams of subjugation, but our currency is still in a deplorable condition. I must say that none of these things interest me in comparison with the interest I feel in everything that concerns my dear parents and friends. You must always tell me everything that is going on with you, do not hide any thing from me, and remember that if you can see positively that I can assist you in your troubles by being in Eng, it is my duty to sacrifice every advantage of position here and return immediately. I trust sincerely that good fortune will soon meet dear father, in his undertakings and that you will be able to give me more cheering accounts when next you write; tell him for me to keep a stout breast and meet all his trials with a determination not to be cast down but to struggle on even to the bitter end. Only think of the misery and desolation of this fair land & all will seem light by comparison. Think of the thousands who have been already slain and of the thousands who may yet be victims to this country's need. Think of the widowed wives, the orphaned children, the bereaved parents; the ruined cities; think of the thousands of women and children who suffer starvation and the bitterest rigors of the elements, while those who ought to be able to remain by their side grasp a musket in the trenches of Petersburg or Richmond. Think of all these things, and bless Almighty God that our own dear England has so long been spared the horrors of an internecine intestine war. Whenever you write I want you to give me all the news concerning father and sister and all my friends. Your letters are a dear consolation to me and each one will keep me in good spirits for a month; there is no difficulty at all in sending them through all my English friends receive letters regularly. You had better continue to send your letters to Maj Walker at Bermuda and doubtles she will forward them, that of Aug 31 came I suppose through him. As I have left Gen Longstreet you must not any longer address as before, let all your future letters be to Capt F. W. Dawson, Gen Fitz Lee's Staff, Care of Mitchel & Tyler, Richmond Va. Mr. Tyler is an intimate friend of mine, indeed I am now staying at his house, and he will take charge of all letters for me as it is very uncertain where I may be, the cavalry moving about all the time. Do you know any thing of Mrs & Miss Allen, I cannot forget their kindness towards me, and I should like very much to hear from them. I have had no letters from Albert or Bartley and only once from Mad. Plaisir. Jog all their memories and ask them to write. Bartley ought to write for the sake of old times, and I am sure that my dear friend Albert has already done so. Give my love to them all. I am very much concerned that sister's education should not be interrupted, I know that you will do all in your power, my noble Mother, would that I could assist you. Tell me is Tetty growing, is she as pretty as ever, and how has she progressed under the tuition of the good Nuns. I am confident that Joey will persevere and perseverance will accomplish any end, tell him that his brother, though separated from him by thousands of weary miles, sends him a kiss and bids him God speed! Dear Parents, and you too dear William, who has been a brother to me in kindness and affection, Christmas is near at hand and will be with you ere this poor letter has crossed the broad Atlantic, remember as you sit together once more around the Christmas table that I am with you in heart, and that on the 25th Dec. as I munch my bacon and bread, or perchance bread alone, among the snow: tipped peaks of the Valley of Virginia, that I shall be thinking of you one and all, my heart aching sadly in vain desire to be with you all again. Tis no use however getting into the blues because I am writing home, through this War I shall go to the end, if I am spared, and then what tales of wars and perils in "the imminent deadly breach" shall I have to tell you, sitting by a comfortable fire and spinning long yarns would be a fit end to the career of a worn out soldier. What is my young friend and your particular star, Andrew Plaisir doing? Let me hear about him. But after all you don't pay much attention to my requests, do you? Long, long, ago I asked for information as to my cousin's address in Baltimore, and Mr. White's address in Piccadilly; and about Miss Bottling, about whom I am of *course breaking my heart although* I daresay she has been married long ago, and not one word have I had from you relative to any of these. Please see the error of your ways and do better in the future. I daresay you have written all about them and that the letters have gone to the bottom. If Mon pere were to write to the Liverpool Agents of Messrs. Fraser Trenholm & Co. of Charleston, I don't know their names, he culd readily ascertain whether they would forward letters; or Mr. White could learn for you how letters are sent to Mr. Vizetelly. There are a dozen different ways of sending letters here regularly and safely, so I hope to hear from you soon. I am very, very anxious to have a letter, and I on my part shall neglect no opportunity of writing.

With fondest love to you and all my relations & friends

> I am
> Your Affectionate Son
> FRANCIS W. DAWSON

> HEAD QUARTERS FITZ: LEE'S DIVISION
> VALLEY OF VIRGINIA, DEC. 17, 1864

My dearest Mother

I received yesterday your letter of October 26, 1864, less than two months after it left England, and I think there is no doubt that two out of every three of your letters will reach me. The news you sent gave me great pleasure, as I when I do not hear from you for a long time, I always fear that some great misfortune may have occurred to you. Bartley's letter has not come and I altogether despair now of receiving it, he must make some mistake in the manner of addressing. Messrs Fraser, Trenholm & Co of Liverpool, and Messrs A. Collie & Co. of Leadenhall St. London are constantly in communication with this country, and I am sure that either of these firms will send letters for you; you had better get father or William to inquire. I know all the agents of Collie & Co. on this side and through one of them I sent you a letter dated about the 25 Nov. in which I gave you all the latest news. Be particular always in naming the dates of my letters which reach you so that I may know what to repeat, and thus save much unnecessary repetition. My position has been entirely changed! On the 10 Nov. Gen Fitz Lee, nephew of Gen R. E. Lee, applied for me to take the place on his staff of one of his Officers who was killed in the Battle of Winchester. Gen Fitz Lee said he wanted a brave man and a good officer and also one whom he could treat as a companion, and that he had heard sufficient of me to justify his selection. Gen Longstreet was very reluctant to give me up but a peremptory order came from Gen R. E. Lee and there was no alternative. I am now then on the Staff of Maj Gen Fitz Lee who is commanding all the cavalry in the Valley of Virginia. The other officers on the Staff are splendid fellows and amongst them is one countryman of mine, Capt Charles Cavendish formerly of the 18th Hussars. In every social relation, my position is as pleasant as it can be, but in other respects cavalry service is no joke. We approach nearer to perpetual motion than anything I had seen previously, we have just returned from a raid across the mountains, the snow was more than a foot deep, the wind howling and screaming about our ears, for miles our road would lie on a narrow ledge, the mountain rising like a wall on our right, while on our left the mountain side fell almost perpendicularly five or six hunderd feet 'till it reached a brook which like a silver thread was winding in the valley below; one slip of the horse, and both man and beast must have tumbled headlong to the bottom of the precipice, yet through such a country as this we wound our way six days without an accident. We have great fun on the raids because they take us into the Yankee lines, and there we meet with red:hot Southerners who receive us with open arms, placing all they have at our disposal. I think the prettiest Lady I have seen in Virginia was one whom we discovered on the last trip, beautiful as a picture, sweet as a peach, graceful and refined, we tired cavalry were as pleased as though we had met the first violet of Spring. Beyond these things we have greater and sterner pleasures, we are not troubled with any long weary manoeuvering before we get into a fight, but so soon as we meet the enemy, away goes a squadron with a cheer driving the picquets back on their reserve, then a Brigade is advanced—and pistol in hand we drive at the blue:coated fiends. As you may well imagine I am no swordsman, and I have to trust entirely to main strength and awkwardness, I am a pretty good shot with a pistol and rely more on that than on anything else. Unless I am knocked over in the meanwhile, I hope to have a good string of "scalps" before the closing of the next campaign. Still in spite of all the "fun", I think the War has lasted quite long enough for me and the people of this Country. I am very anxious to see it over, but we *can not, dare* not give up, and Lincoln has no idea of relinquishing his claims as you may see by his Message. In men and munitions of war we are strong enough to meet any efforts the Yankees may make, but our financial affairs are in terrible confusion. My month's pay ought to be worth £30 and in Confederate money as we receive it, that would just buy *one Boot*, it wd take two months to buy a pair; is not this rich in the extreme. Still do not be uneasy about me, I have every comfort that I need and want particularly for nothing. I am very glad that you were pleased with the specimens of Confederate money. I enclose some more, they are paid to us as being equal to gold or silver, but it takes now forty (40) dollars Confederate to buy a gold dollar. From and after the receipt of this letter, address to me as follows:—Capt Francis W. Dawson, Maj Gen Fitz Lee's Staff, Care of Messrs. Mitchell and Tyler, Richmond Va. You had better address so, as now I am so constantly moving about that I cannot give any certain address in the Field. You must send the kindest possible message to Albert and all my friends for me, I hope still to have a happy re:union in old England. As for Bartley I will never forgive him unless he writes and tells me all the news. Do not spoil Lassie too much as I shall not be able to do anything with her again. William needs no thanks I know for his constant acts of kindness, still tell him how deeply grateful I am for anything done for any of you. Give him my best love, and tell him to enjoy himself at Christmas for *two*. Why does not Father write, I hope he may be too busy to have time, that is the only way that I can excuse it. I hope you have ere this received my likeness, or I must try to get another for you. Give my best love to every one, including the children &

Believe me to remain
Your affectionate child
FRANCIS W. DAWSON

HEAD QUARTERS LEE'S CAV DIVISION
DEC. 25. 1864

My dearest Mother,

A few days ago I recd your letter of Oct 26 and immediately sent a reply to Wilmington, but my friend Capt Cavendish tells me that he will start for England in a day or two and I cannot lose the opportunity of writing to you again. This is Christmas day, dear Mother, and doubtless as you sat around your dinner table at home in quiet Isleworth you have thought and talked of your absent son. You are always present in my mind and more particularly on such a day as this when we have been accustomed to meet at our home. For the past ten days we have been riding nearly night and day to check the movements of the Yankee cavalry who were making a raid on Gordonsville and I have been pretty nearly worn out. On Tuesday we marched all night, we had already gone 30 miles since morning, the snow was falling in small flakes mixed with hail which froze as it touched your clothes, my hat was as stiff as a board, icicles hanging all around the brim, my coat shining with ice, my horse slipping and sliding at every step, we started at 1 oclock in the morning and rode fourteen miles before we struck the Yankee camp, we had but 500 men and there were 3000 Yanks, we got within 200 yds of their fires about break of day, formed our troops and with a yell and shout charged right down on them, it was a perfect surprise, and after a short fight drove them off in headlong confusion. Our loss was very slight and we captured a number of horses and prisoners. A bullet struck me on the leg, cutting my trousers and drawers and just breaking the skin, so much for luck. Yesterday Gen Lee gave me permission to come down to Richmond to spend Christmas, and I have thus the opportunity of quietly writing this. My friends in Richmond are particularly kind to me. I have always a home here at Mr. Tyler's whenever I come to town. I know not how to appreciate sufficiently the uniform courtesy and consideration which has been extended to me. Your last letter gave me great satisfaction, and I was delighted to find that affairs were no worse with you. I had been very anxious, but I now hope that with the blessing of Providence father will be able to surmount all his difficulties and see his way clear to a comparatively prosperous career. I feel very deeply all father's troubles and trials. I know how much he has still struggled on, tell him from me that I am with him heart and soul in all his labors, and beg him always and often to write to me and tell me all that he is doing, all his plans and all his intentions, don't let me think that I am estranged from you because I am not in England, don't let me think that distance or time makes me any the less your affectionate Son. Thanks for your news from Bartley, I have not yet received his letter, tell him I shall not forgive him until I receive a letter with all the news. Henceforth direct my letters as follows, Capt Francis W. Dawson, Maj. Gen. Fitz:Lee's Staff, care of Messrs. Mitchell & Tyler, Richmond, Virginia. C.S.A. You can send through Major Walker, or Messrs Fraser, Trenholm & Co of Liverpool, or Messrs A. Collie & Co. of Leadenhall St will I am sure send on your letters. Perhaps William will call on Messrs Collie and ask them, their ships are coming over constantly and and it would be a safe and expeditious channel for you.

Our affairs here just now are as blue as indigo, in Georgia everything seems to go wrong, in Virginia alone Confederate arms maintain their own ground position, but a brighter day will soon come and we shall be able soon to recover our lost ground and show Europe that the South is still able to conquer and maintain her independence. Tis sad, sad, indeed to see the ruin and desolation which now reign in some of the most beautiful portions of this once happy land, no man, whatever his fortune, is safe, a Yankee raid may in an hour make beggars of the richest: not a family but has lost some near and dear one, how then can the North or England think, that we shall be willing to allow all these fearful sacrifices to be made in vain; how could we affilliate with those who have murdered brothers, fathers, sons, who have reduced thousands of affluent families to beggary; shall we brand ourselves as recreant cowards by relinquishing the contest: shall we disgrace the memory of the thousands who have fallen, by allowing now that we have been persecuting an unholy and unjustifiable war: No! whatever our disaster the South can never give up, we must struggle, still struggle to the last.

Your letters can never be uninteresting to me so long as they contain news from home, do not fear then that the details of your quiet domestic life have no attraction for me. I like to know all that is going on at home. I don't expect you to write of wars and rumours of wars, of political debates and party struggles. I have enough of those here, all that I want is news, news of home. William is I am sure treading unswervingly his path in life, may he always be as prosperous as he deserves, his kindness to you and the children has placed me under a debt towards him beyond any repayment that I hope to make I wish he would write to me. Tell Joe to work on and work hard during the golden hours of youth, and he will hereafter reap a rich harvest from his labors, whatever his future career in life, his success will and must depend on the use he makes of the time and opportunity he can now command. Kiss sister for me, tell her that if by God's blessing I live till the war is over, I will certainly go home again, if only for a month or two. Give my kindest regards to the Plaisirs, tell them I could write to them separately, but I am moving about all the time and, as many of my letters, may miscarry I wish as frequently as possible, to write to you. Send me the address of my cousin Mr. White in Baltimore, and the *No* of Mr. White's firm in London, if I should accidentally be taken prisoner Mr. W. of Baltimore might be of great assistance to me. Do not forget in each of your letters to mention the dates of the last 3 or 4 letters you have had from me, so that I may know which have been lost and what news to repeat.

Thank Mother Teresa and the good nuns and *Granny* for their kindness and prayers, beg of them still to pray for me, to your prayers and theirs, under God, do I alone attribute the safety which has hitherto attended me.

With re:iterated assurances of affection and sympathy

Believe me to remain, My dear father & mother,

Your affectionate Son

FRANCIS W. DAWSON

Cap & c

P.S.   Ask Mr. Steel to write, give him my kindest regards.

PETERSBURG VA. JUNE 5, 1865

My dear Mother:

Yesterday evening I returned to Town from Mecklenberg County, where I had been on a visit to Dr. Jones a son:in:law of Mr. Raines, and found a whole budget of letters dated early in May and which had been awaiting me some time;—The letters were from you and father, Joey, Mad Plaisir, & Bartley, each of these will be answered in a day or two.

When I first wrote you from Richmond my wound was in a very precarious condition, but, it began rapidly to improve, examinations were made by the first Surgeons in our Army and they decided that as the ball had lodged under the muscles of the shoulder and seemed to give me no inconvenience that it should not be interfered with. The wound is now entirely healed and I am happy to say that it causes me no inconvenience, barring an absence of great muscular power, and severe occasional twinges of pain in damp weather. So that I can afford now to laugh at my wounds, and thank God heartily that I have in His mercy been spared.

I fully appreciate, dear Mother, all that you say concerning my return to Eng., my heart aches to see you, and I know the tender and affectionate greeting I should meet with at all your hands, but you must appreciate my position. As an Officer of Gen. R. E. Lee's Army, although not present at the surrender, I was entitled to and received my parole. I am now on parole and not *allowed to leave the Country*, I could cancel the parole and free myself by taking the Oath of Allegiance to the U.S. Govt. but this I am most unwilling to do, as so soon as a British Consul comes to Richmond I shall endeavour to obtain protection as a British Subject. Beyond this there is a more terrible difficulty. I have not a sixpence in the World and at present I cannot obtain any. Confederate money I had an abundance of but that is only valuable as waste paper, and my three riding horses which I left in Camp when I was wounded were all taken by the Yanks although had I been present I could have saved them. My friends although they are wealthy men are in much the same condition as myself, but they have cotton and tobacco on hand which will put them in funds as soon [as] the markets open. I can then, that is to say in a few months, get the necessary sinews of war from them. Beyond all doubt this would be a better place in which for me to begin the World afresh than Eng. Judging by the condition of things here prior to the War, salaries are *higher* and *cost of living* less. So that I thought of endeavouring to obtain safe employment here or in Richmond if only of a temporary character, although at present it is almost impossible to do anything. The wealthy merchants have in most cases been heavy sufferers by the fall of our Country, and many of them are not able to resume their old business, while in addition the town is over:run by swarms of miserable Yankee traders who have their own hirelings with them. If then some windfall does not come it seems to me that I shall at least have to remain here until I can earn enough to carry be back to Old Eng. I would give anything only to be able to be with you, if for a few days even, I am so anxious to see you all, remember that although I have many kind friends here that for four years and more I have not heard the voice of father, mother, sister, brother or any relation of my own.

From father's letter I shd judge that he is going on more prosperously now than at any time within my recollection. Surely the blessing of Heaven will be upon his labors; he is so persevering & self-denying and has been ever so faithful and diligent, that, by every law human or divine, he ought to succeed. A great anxiety has been raised from my heart by his good news and I feel more at ease now than I have done at any time during the last two years. Mad P. tells me that you are looking very well, and not at all older in appearance than when I left home; I am heartily glad to hear it, you must take care of yourself that I may see you looking the same dear Mother of former days.

I grieve very much that Uncle Tom has been so unfortunate: how did he continue to lose his money? Give my love and sympathies to them all. It seems very droll to me that Joey should be able to write me such a genial and sensible letter. I cannot realise the difference that four years must have made. Joe gets on the stilts occasionally but tis a fault common to young letter writers. As for myself I do [not] believe that I am in the least changed, and I am sure that you will say that I am the same good for nothing sort of person in appearance that I was at home. My face is as smooth as ever, and I never could get up a fierce and soldierly beard. I had two likenesses taken for you and sent them over by Mrs. & Mr. Cameron of Petersburg who left this place two months ago; I hear that they have been to Eng and are now in Ireland, so surely you will receive them, they also carried with them a plain wooden pipe for father, the only claim to interest of which is that it was made by a Confederate soldier in the Trenches. All my little relics were left in Camp when I came away and were captured by the Yanks when I was wounded, including my sabre and pistol, I had the sense to put my trunk in the ambulance and carry it on with me so that my clothes were saved, but I omitted to bring my private desk and that was the severest loss of all, all my commissions in the service, many interesting official papers, and two *diaries* wh[ich] would have been as interesting as Romances and more true, were all lost, and had I not the other day taken the precaution to obtain a certificate of my rank from Gen Fitz Lee I cd not have proved myself to a stranger a Confederate Officer. As the War is over now and I am more likely to incur danger from chimney-pots and trees, than bullets and sabres, it is no harm to tell you that the profession of a soldier would be my choice above, far above, any other occupation with which I am acquainted. To me there is a singular fascination in all a soldier's trials and hardships, and I feel now that I would go a hundred miles to get into a fight; but don't be alarmed I am on parole and there is no fighting to do. You made a very amusing mistake concerning "Miss White" that "dear young lady" who last night showed me your letter to her. I know that you thought I had been gathering myself a sweet-heart in this Country, but alas! this side of the Atlantic can never contain a sweet-heart of mine. But Miss White who is a singular niece of Capt Pegram has been married ten or twelve years to a most estimable and wealthy citizen of Petersburg and has a family of three charming children. Still so far as appearances go she is as youthful and fresh as a young maiden of sixteen; she is a true pure hearted Southern lady, and has a fascination and charm in her manners which is as rare as it is bewitching. *Mrs* White has always been and always will be a firm and true friend of mine; she is extremely pretty, is as graceful as a fawn, has an exquisite figure, and, were she unmarried, my heart or a corner of it would have been lost long since; as it is she is a dear kind sister to me. Mr. White was one of the most wealthy men in the State but I fear that he has suffered very heavily—I know that he lost about £20,000 in tobacco alone when Petersburg was evacuated. Mrs. White will answer your letter at once, when you write to her, address to *Mrs* I. A. White, Petersburg, *Va*, U.S.A.

You don't tell me whether sister Tetty is changed at all and whether she is as pretty as ever. I should very much like to have her likeness,— Joe's went off with the rest of my relics. Did, you ever receive the photograph which I sent you? it was not at all flattering, so folks say, but it would have given you an idea of the uniform. Tell William to write to me and not to stand upon any ceremony, but tell him I am so "hard up" that he must pay the postage, so you will all for the present have the double benefit of paying postage both ways. Thank Goodness I did contrive to save my uniform altho' somewhat faded and I can have another likeness taken for you if you do not receive any of the others. Is Mr. Steel still at Woodlands? If so ask him to write. You must give my love to all my friends and relations general and particular, and thank the Revd Mother and Sisters for their kindness and prayers, if I have been spared in this War it was not by my own deserts; and I have to thank God's mercy and your entreaties to Him for that life which is only valuable to me as it may enable me to serve and aid you when the frosts of age silver my dear parents' brows.

With fondest Love to you all
I remain
Your Affectionate Son
FRANCIS W. DAWSON

Address to
Messrs. Mitchell & Tyler
Main St.
Richmond, Va *U.S.A.*

[P.S.] What is Lance doing; he was not *honest*, have you ever heard anything of the Haskins or Allens?

NOTES

1 For a brief sketch of the *Nashville* and her exploits in Confederate service, see John T. Scharf, *History of the Confederate States Navy* (Albany, N.Y.: n.p., 1894), 795–96.

2 Captain Robert P. Pegram, Virginia naval officer, nephew of General John W. Pegram of the Confederate Army.

3 Lieutenant James H. North, Confederate naval agent sent to England in the spring of 1861 to arrange for the procurement of ironclad battleships.

4 Captain Frederick Marryat, English naval officer and novelist, who visited the United States in 1837 and recorded his experiences and impressions in *A Diary in America with Remarks on Its Institutions,* published in two volumes in Philadelphia in 1839.

5 Frederick Chemier was the author of *The Life of a Sailor* published in London in 1850.

6 Richard H. Dana's *Two Years Before the Mast* was published in Boston in 1911.

7 The exploits of the *Virginia* at Hampton Roads, including the fight with the Federal *Monitor*, are recounted in William C. Davis, *Duel between the First Ironclads* (New York: Doubleday, 1975).

8 Probably Major Benjamin W. Belches, Thirteenth Virginia Cavalry Regiment, C.S.A.

9 The name of this installation, the construction of which was begun in 1819, was officially changed on February 1, 1832, from Fortress Monroe to Fort Monroe. However, the original name was widely used throughout the Civil War and afterward.

10 Forts Jackson and St. Philip surrendered to the Federals on April 28, 1862.

11 According to Charles L. Dufour, *The Night the War Was Lost* (New York: Doubleday, 1960), 325–26, the *Louisiana* was destroyed on April 28, 1862, by a huge explosion of powder from flames set by her crew to prevent the vessel from being captured by the Federals.

12 Constance (Cary) Harrison's wartime experiences are recounted in her book *Recollections Grave and Gay* published by Charles Scribner's Sons in 1911.

13 The Gatling gun, named for its inventor, Richard Gatling, was a multibarrel small caliber, rapid-fire weapon operated by turning a crank. It had only limited use during the Civil War.

14   The book referred to is John J. Craven, *The Prison Life of Jefferson Davis* (New York: Carlton, 1866) .

15   Letters and diaries of Confederate soldiers written during the Gettysburg campaign indicate that General Lee's prohibitory orders were sometimes cheerfully ignored. See Bell I. Wiley, *The Life of Johnny Reb: The Common Soldier of the Confederacy* (Indianapolis: Bobbs-Merrill, 1943) , 47.

16   FitzGerald Ross's Confederate experiences were published in 1864–1865 as a series of articles in *Blackwood's Magazine* and in 1865 in a book entitled *A Visit to the Cities and Camps of the Confederate States*. For Vizetelly's Confederate experiences, see W. Stanley Hoole (ed.) , *Vizetelly Covers the Confederacy* (Tuscaloosa, Ala., 1957) .

17   Ella Lonn, in *Foreigners in the Confederacy* (Chapel Hill, 1940) , 185, gives Winthrop's English unit as the 22nd Regiment Foot.

18   For Sorrel's Confederate experiences see G. Moxley Sorrell, *Recollections of a Confederate Staff Officer,* ed. Bell I. Wiley (Jackson, Tenn.: McCowat-Mercer, 1958.)